FINDING SHALOM

ALSO BY KIRK BLACKARD

Change in a Unionized Workplace: Countervailing Collaboration

Capitalizing on Conflict: Strategies and Practices for Turning Conflict to Synergy (with James W. Gibson)

Restoring Peace: Using Lessons from Prison to Mend Broken Relationships

Makin It: A Story of Hope (illustrated by Ben Humenik)

Reconciling the Bible and Science: A Primer on the Two Books of God (with Dr. Lynn Mitchell)

Burrs, Bull Nettles, and Bare Feet: Stories of a Country Childhood

Face to Face: Our Story of Crime, Repentance, and Forgiveness (with Keith Blackburn and Misty Wright)

Love in a cauldron of misery: perspectives on Christian prison ministry

Nurturing Peace: How Families can Help Incarcerated Loved Ones Change Their Lives

A Tale of Conflict and Peace at the B Bar Ranch

Stuff I've Done and Things I've Learned: Musings of a Grateful Grandad

Stop Abuse and Transform Your Life: Homework for Battering Intervention (with Francesca Blackard and Albert Chagoya)

Betrayed by Choices: A Family Story of Murder, Forgiveness, and Redemption (with Jim Buffington, Jr.)

FINDING SHALOM

*Journeys
Beyond
Peace*

KIRK BLACKARD

FOREWORD BY JOHN SAGE,
FOUNDER AND EXECUTIVE DIRECTOR, BRIDGES TO LIFE

ISBN: 979-8-218-56914-3
Cover and book design by Mayfly book design

Library of Congress Catalog Number: 2024925851

First Printing: 2025

FOREWORD

It is an often sad but inevitable part of the human experience that we will go through life-changing events. Such events impact us in various ways and to varying degrees, but in their wake, our lives are never the same again. Having the benefit of thirty-one years of hindsight and reflection, I can tell you that my most significant life-changing event occurred on June 30, 1993. That was the day my sister Marilyn was brutally murdered by two nineteen-year-old strangers. For Marilyn, it was a random event of being at the wrong place at the wrong time, encountering the wrong people. For her family—Marilyn's children, mother, and seven siblings—it was a tragedy of overwhelming magnitude, leaving us shattered, heartbroken, and grieving.

I consider my time on earth before June 30, 1993 to be my "old life"; after that date, my new life began. I was broken and I longed to be rescued from this season of anguish and pain. In my search for answers, I stumbled across an Ernest Hemingway quote: *"The world breaks everyone. And afterward, some are strong at the broken places."* These words ignited in me a passionate pursuit of exactly how a person can become strong at the broken places. I spent the next five years meditating and studying the concepts of personal surrender to God, humility, God's love for me, acceptance, gratitude, forgiveness, and helping others. I believe these five years, along with a strong Christian faith and God's helping hand, became the core of my personal journey to peace, and ultimately led me to the founding of Bridges To Life.

Kirk Blackard's book, *Finding Shalom: Journeys Beyond Peace*, explores life at an even higher level than peace. Most of us are aware that "shalom" is the Jewish word for peace, but it was not until I read *Finding Shalom* that I began to understand the deeper meaning and value of the concept of shalom. As a long-time volunteer for Bridges To Life, Kirk uses stories about our program's inmate and volunteer participants to demonstrate ways for you to listen to God and discern his will, live with love, faith, and hope, and take actions that can lead you to higher levels in your spiritual life. I think Kirk has given us a valuable road map to finding shalom and journeys beyond peace.

John Sage
Founder/CEO, Bridges To Life

CONTENTS

INTRODUCTION

*The Lord bless you and keep you; the Lord make his face
to shine upon you and be gracious to you; the Lord lift up his
countenance upon you and give you peace.*
(Numbers 26:24–26).

I committed to three goals upon retirement after a thirty-year career with Shell Oil Company. The first was to write a book and have it published. My first book, *Managing Change in a Unionized Workplace*, may have won the year's award for the best sleep aid on the market. My second goal was to quit embarrassing myself so much in golf. I felt I could say, with somewhat reasonable honesty, that I was making some, although limited, progress. My third goal was to do more community service work than I had done in the past. Progress toward this goal was not going well. I had joined the board of directors of an organization dealing with addiction, but resigned when I became concerned about the possibility of it being involved in some financial improprieties.

I was still looking for a place to serve when my wife, Marcia, and I were invited to a friend's birthday party. Midway through the evening I ran into John Sage, who I had become acquainted with when he was my son Chris's soccer coach approximately five years before. After the obligatory small talk, John mentioned that his sister, Marilyn, had been brutally murdered several years before by two Houston nineteen-year-olds. He said this had triggered him to establish a faith-based prison ministry called Bridges To Life, and he was its executive director.

After we had discussed more details of the crime and ministry, John posed his inevitable question: "Would you consider volunteering in a prison, working with a small group of inmates much like those who murdered Marilyn?"

I began volunteering as a small group facilitator at the "Walls" unit in Huntsville shortly after my encounter with John. After completing this project and several others, I could see how the Bridges To Life experience fostered a significant level of healing and peace among victims of crime and convicted felons who had committed such crimes; and I came to believe that the process also would work for those who in lesser but significant ways had offended or been offended by strangers, business associates, friends, relatives, or loved ones. This led to my writing *Restoring Peace: Using Lessons From Prison to Mend Broken Relationships*, which presented the BTL process as a way to restore broken relationships among anyone who was experiencing them. Although its aim was to minimize conflict and foster peace, harmony, and tranquility among any individuals experiencing strife and seeking peace in their lives, the book became a centerpiece of the BTL curriculum,

By the time of this writing in 2024, roughly 85,000 men and women, with the help of 3,800 volunteers, have completed the BTL program since its inception. Most have made dramatic changes in their lives, and many have found a state of shalom from which all of us can learn. *Finding Shalom: Journeys Beyond Peace* shares many of their experiences and learnings.

"Shalom," used widely as a greeting in communities around the world, often is equated with peace, defined as the absence of conflict and freedom from fear of violence in relationships, or as serenity before God. However, shalom embodies a deeper meaning. It includes serenity before God and peace, but also wholeness, completeness, health, welfare, safety, tranquility, contentment, soundness, prosperity, and rest.

Finding Shalom: Journeys Beyond Peace picks up where *Restoring Peace* left off and aims to foster shalom for anyone who is dealing with conflict, suffering life difficulties, or just wants a better life. It draws from published works of prominent people in the appropriate fields; stories of crime perpetrators, victims, and alcohol and drug abusers who have changed their lives; other individuals who have changed and built lives that are by and large characterized by shalom; and some of my personal experiences. The book posits that you can find shalom if you intentionally and purposefully look for it by doing things that are good and worthwhile standing alone, and that will in combination cause shalom to ensue.

Chapters 1 and 2 explore ways for you to listen to God and discern his will.

Chapters 3 through 5 consider love, faith, and hope—sometimes considered the three graces—and how they foster shalom.

The remaining Chapters, 6 through 11, consider individual actions you can take to transform your life and find shalom.

Peace is a critical aspect of shalom, but it only begins to scratch the surface of the richness of the concept. Peace, and the role of peace in shalom, is a little like the foundation of a house. One of many parts comprising the whole, the foundation typically is not seen, and the remainder of the house is built on it. Without it, the house crumbles, but with a good foundation, a house can be a thing of service and beauty for years. The foundation can only be designed after one knows what the house will look like, but it is the first part to be constructed. Similarly, peace is the foundation of shalom. If peace exists, it is usually not seen, but if it is not present, conflict or fear of conflict makes a life of shalom impossible.

Shalom is a response to needs that stands squarely against injustice and oppression, and is clearly on the side of salvation for the weak, the poor, the grieving, and the disenfranchised. Shalom is active, with parties working to find common ground, maintain relationships, and live fulfilling lives. It is characterized by three basic dimensions of meaning.

First, living in right relationship with others and with God is the way in which shalom is used that is closest to the way peace is usually used. This dimension contemplates good, regulated, normal relationships between nations, groups, or individuals or between individuals and God. It describes relationships that are right, positive, and good—not just an absence of conflict or tolerating one another—and that are maintained in the face of physical separation and alienation. Romans 12:16-18 defines it as follows: "Live in harmony with one another. . . . If it is possible, as far as it depends on you, live at peace with everyone."

Shalom also means material, mental, and physical well-being. Life is all right, okay, sometimes even in abundance. If people are to find shalom, they must strive to bring physical, mental, or material well-being into their lives and the lives of those who do not now enjoy it. Most prison inmates have endured many unmet needs in their past lives and have never experienced shalom. People who are locked in cages were rarely physically, mentally, and materially okay before they were locked up. By and large, they have never been okay. They are often the poor, the undereducated, the mentally challenged, the small-time drug dealers and thugs who live on the margins of society. While they are in prison, they often face a brutal environment that is far from okay. Victims of crime are not in a state of well-being or all-rightness, but instead typically are filled with fear, pain, grief, and other emotions that are difficult to describe. And many others suffer their own unique difficulties. Material well-being requires a significant change in all their lives.

The third meaning of shalom is honesty, integrity, and straightforwardness—the opposite of deceit, lies, evil, guilt, and hypocrisy. This is the moral element of shalom. Zechariah 8:14 says, "These are the things you are to do: Speak the truth to each other, and render true and sound judgment in your courts; do not plot evil against your neighbor, and do not love to swear falsely. 'I hate all this,' declares the Lord." Christian morality says that the best way to behave is to live in keeping with the teaching of Jesus and adhere to the moral codes of the Bible, such as the Ten Commandments, the Sermon on the Mount, and the Golden Rule. It involves a sense of behavior that distinguishes between right and wrong, good and bad or evil, and guides people's choices. The presence of morality is indicated by how people behave rather than by what they think or believe. Personal morality comes from many sources: family, schools, the culture and society in which people have lived, religion and the teaching of religious leaders, the actions of role models, people's experiences and what they have observed others experience, and on and on. From all this, we choose, either consciously or by default, the ones that apply to our lives and make us who we are.

Vietnamese Zen Buddhist monk Thich Nhat Hahn (1926–2022) taught that each person has within them both seeds of peace and seeds of violence. Which of the seeds grows depends on which seed the person chooses to water. Many contemporary influences nurture the seeds of violence, but if we water the seeds of peace, we can journey toward shalom. We can blossom like a flower and everyone in our family and in our society will benefit from our actions. I hope the ideas shared in this book will be the water that helps you journey to find shalom in your life. You can start by listening to God.

Questions for Reflection

1. Why are you reading *Finding Shalom*? What do you hope to get from it?
2. What do you need for a better life?
3. Which aspect of shalom is most meaningful to you?

1

LISTENING TO GOD

But He said, "On the contrary, blessed are those who
hear the word of God and observe it."
(Luke 11:28)

Debbie Mosley explained, "I decided I would just have a car wreck on Highway 45, so I started driving toward Galveston, looking for a concrete pillar that I could crash my car into and kill myself. I was crying hysterically and that's when my life changed. I heard this man's voice in the back seat of my car. In a loud clear voice, he told me that he loved me and that I would always be his child."

Debbie ran head-on into a situation involving listening to God rather than a concrete pillar.

Most people have not heard God's voice with the clarity and certainty Debbie described, and you probably never will, but you can do things that help. You can pay attention to the "synchronicity" in your life, and you can thoughtfully and intentionally do several things from which you are likely to hear His word.

SYNCHRONICITY

"Synchronicity" describes one way of listening to God. Renowned Swiss psychologist, Carl Jung, who introduced the concept, defined synchronicity as a meaningful coincidence of two or more events that appear to be unrelated but are experienced together. Although the events do not have a cause-and-effect relationship, their occurrence together is seen as having great significance or meaning. Synchronicity involves events that are improbable, difficult to explain, and often seem to be accidental. It refers to events that mysteriously occur in one's life that seem to be highly symbolic and meaningful. If serendipity or coincidence is like a bread crumb, synchronicity is like a trail of crumbs that leads one toward a new destination.

The events occurring in the aftermath of the murder of John Sage's sister, during the founding of Bridges To Life, and in the writing of *Restoring Peace* provide examples in abundance.

John's rage and grief over Marilyn's death were indescribable, and seemingly never-ending. A few months after her death, still in the depths of despair, John started crying and fell to his knees on his cold bathroom floor. He pleaded, "God, just tell me what to do."

A voice seemed to answer, "Just give it to me, John."

He prayed, "God, I can't go on like this. I'm letting go and trusting you to be in charge of my life. I surrender."

A man and a woman were tried, convicted, and sent to death row for his sister's murder, but this didn't bring Marilyn back, and it didn't alleviate John's feeling of despair, hopelessness, and depression. He couldn't move on, and he couldn't get his life back. He began to wonder if he had really let go, trusted God, and given it all to him as he had promised.

The man died in prison after four years of incarceration. Approximately five years after the crime and three years after her trial and conviction, the woman told prosecutors, for reasons known only to her, that she wanted to waive her appeal and be executed. Her execution was set for April 20, 1998. (Reverend Jesse Jackson intervened, and she withdrew her request to be executed and continued the appeal process.)

Her scheduled death set in motion a series of events that at the time seemed to be merely coincidental or serendipitous, but upon reflection appear far more significant, and have formed a trail leading to the founding and success of the Bridges To Life ministry. The first event was a phone call.

Early in 1998, John received a call from a reporter for the *ABC 20/20* news magazine. After they exchanged brief introductions, she said, "Your sister's killer has an execution date in a few months. Are you excited?".

John replied, "Honestly, no I'm not."

"But this awful woman. You can watch her get the lethal injection. Wouldn't it feel good?"

"No. It would not feel good. If you're looking for someone to be excited about seeing drugs injected into another person to kill them, you are at the wrong place."

"I'm amazed you're not even angry," the reporter snapped as she abruptly hung up. She said she would call back, but never did.

John was amazed as well. He was struck by his feeling that sometime during the previous year, he had let go of much of his anger and desire for revenge and put his life in God's hands.

A few weeks after the call, John mentioned his conversation to Diane Clements, leader of a local victim's advocate group involved with the "Sycamore Tree" program—a volunteer-led, twelve-week victim awareness program for incarcerated offenders. This conversation piqued John's interest, as he had been considering ways to better deal with his personal trauma and prevent the tragedy that happened in his family from happening to others, by helping offenders change. He concluded that the greatest concentration of potential offenders needing change was in the prisons, so that was perhaps where his effort should be focused. Soon thereafter, he started volunteering at Jester 2 unit, now the Carol Vance Prison.

John then got a consulting contract to develop a reentry program for Prison Fellowship, the large Christian nonprofit organization for prisoners, former prisoners, and their families, founded in 1976 by Charles W. Colson, a former Richard Nixon aide who served a seven-month prison sentence for a Watergate-related crime. The contract allowed John to stay involved and learn more about inmates and prisons—for minimal pay.

That fall John attended a conference where he met several Victim Services staff, heard more about prison issues, and reflected on his future. Among the people he encountered was Ellen Halbert, a former TDCJ board member who, not coincidentally, had a prison named after her, and Ronnie Earle, the Travis County District Attorney. During a breakfast conversation, John mentioned that he was considering starting a prison program centered on victim impact. After hearing more about John's plans, both were supportive. Ellen said she would like to be on the board of directors and an advisor if he started this nonprofit corporation. John considered this to be a profound gesture for a plan that had never been implemented and was still in the concept stage.

Driving from Dallas back to Houston that night, the question of whether he should start a prison ministry kept reverberating through John's mind. Finally, he had all he could take and somewhere on Highway 45 he said to himself and to God, "OK God. You're gonna have your way, one way or the other. So, I'm going to just try it." To borrow a phrase, John had reached that point "where freedom and destiny merge."

The next week, John told his friend, Phillip Burguieres, about his plans to start a nonprofit corporation to deliver victim impact programs to incarcerated offenders. Phillip agreed on the spot to arrange funding of half the budget for the first year. A lawyer friend donated legal work to incorporate Bridges To Life as a 501(c)(3) organization. A member of John's Bible study group suggested a "vision luncheon" to explain the plans and raise more money, and within thirty days a luncheon for forty-five people, funded by Phillip, was held and more money and support came in.

All of this happened within sixty days, as John continued with Sycamore Tree-like meetings of victims and offenders. He began developing curriculum, doing the writing just in time, one session at a time, one week before each inmate/victim meeting. He completed the Sycamore Tree project and then took a handful of volunteers to the Leblanc unit in Beaumont for the first Bridges To Life program. *Restoring Peace: Using Lessons From Prison to Mend Broken Relationships* further developed the topics John had initiated.

My writing of *Restoring Peace* continued the trail of synchronicity as an important part of Bridges To Life.

I'm not sure why Marcia and I were invited to the party where I reconnected with John and agreed to become a BTL volunteer. We were acquaintances of the birthday boy, but not close friends. We would not have expected to be invited to the party, but we were.

I was interested in a volunteer opportunity only because I had the unproven, unsubstantiated "feeling" that there might be some financial irregularities in the organization where I had been volunteering and decided to resign from its board.

I had never thought about writing a book based on Bridges To Life. The idea of doing so popped into my head—seemingly out of the blue—as I sat half asleep in a van of volunteers returning from Beaumont to Houston. My freedom and destiny merged immediately, and John agreed to the book within a matter of days.

During the writing, when I seemed to be developing writer's block trying to figure out how to deal with or explain a particular issue, a BTL offender or volunteer at a weekly session would almost always jump in on que, without any knowledge at all that I was even writing a book, and provide an answer for me.

I "coincidentally" connected with several people during the writing who I did not know, who willingly shared their time and expertise and had major influences on the book. Three were particularly helpful. I met Sam Todd, Episcopal priest and author, on the Herman Park golf course, and he later advised me on several theological questions, and in particular the issue of forgiving self. An acquaintance connected me with Evelyn Nolen from the staff of Rice University, who edited the writing for no charge. Carol Vance, former chairman of the board of the Texas Department of Criminal Justice, suggested over lunch that *Restoring Peace* be used as part of the BTL curriculum.

We found a company on Google who prints the book (approximately 100,000 copies at the time of this writing) at a price that makes it feasible to give copies to all BTL participants.

Events of synchronicity such as these have continued to run throughout the life of Bridges To Life.

Views vary as to why such things happen and how synchronicity occurs. Some say it is a form of confirmation bias, where we see what we believe rather than believe what we see. Others believe it is simply a habit of seeing connections and patterns in random and/or meaningless data, while still others think synchronicity comes from the unconscious mind.

Synchronicities are magical events that can nourish and encourage your faith and remind you that you aren't alone; you are connected, and there is a mysterious and meaningful direction to your life. One of the great spiritual lessons that synchronicity teaches is the idea of surrender. When we surrender, we do our part and then step aside and "let go and let God." This allows synchronicities into our life and things start to unfold naturally. People of faith generally believe synchronicity is a sign from their Higher Self or an intervention from God. He is sending them messages, often called "divine providence," with wisdom and love, that direct their lives in ways they cannot explain and that embrace mystery more than logic. Squire Rushnell calls it "Godwinks" in his book, *When God Winks: How the Power of Coincidence Guides Your Life.*

I know of no objective way to determine whether synchronicity is God's providence or just plain 'ole' luck. A person's belief boils down to opinion, experience, flexible definitions, and one's belief about God. I'm pretty sure I can't explain exactly how God works in people's lives, but I'm also pretty sure I can see the synchronicity in John's life, in the founding of Bridges To Life, in the writing of *Restoring Peace*, and in the organization's growth over the years.

Those who believe God has a hand in such things are in good company. Carl Jung maintained that "invoked or not invoked, God is present."[1] And Albert Einstein has said, "Coincidence is God's way of staying anonymous."[2]

I am convinced that synchronicity is not an accident, and I believe people can identify, understand, and affect its frequency in their lives. Stuff happens to those who are present. Good things happen to those who work to help themselves and others. God answers the prayers of those who pray. In the words of Archbishop of Canterbury William Temple, "All I know is the more I pray, the more coincidences there are in my life."[3] You can do many things that increase the probability of events happening in your life that restore peace and foster shalom.

INTENTIONALITY

Really listening to God requires hard work and attentiveness. A starting point is to study the Bible and pray, which fills your mind with the words, thoughts, and images of Scripture and deepens your connection with Him. There is no guarantee that you will hear the voice or discern the direction of God regarding a specific issue, but sometimes God speaks to you in words you hear as though from Him. For example, an idea, voice, or a picture might pop into your mind when running alone or driving a car in solitude.

A prayer for discernment and wisdom helps you not only to make decisions that are right for you, but also to connect to a higher power. Such a prayer encourages spiritual and emotional growth and can provide the clarity and direction you need to make decisions that are in your best interest. It is a powerful tool to help you stay focused on your goals, and to make decisions that align with your values. Prayer can provide you with the strength and guidance needed to make wise choices and connect meaningfully with your faith, to find the courage and clarity to make decisions that are in your and others' best interest, and to trust in a higher power for support.

In *Discernment: Reading the Signs of Daily Life*, Henri Nouwen (1932-1996), a Dutch Catholic priest, professor, writer, and theologian describes discernment as divine guidance resulting from "a spiritual understanding and an experiential knowledge of how God is active in daily life that is acquired through disciplined spiritual practice ."[4] Nouwen says, "To discern means first of all to listen to God, to pay attention to God's active presence, and to obey God's prompting, direction, leading, and guidance."[5]

Nouwen says you can listen to God through the books you read, the nature you enjoy, the people you meet, and the events you experience.

Books

Neuwen says that as we read spiritually about spiritual things, we open our hearts to God's voice, and sometime we must be willing to put down the book we are reading to just listen to what God is saying to us through its words.

My earliest recollection of reading books is sometime around the fourth grade, and my interest continues today. Most of the effect of my reading has been bit-by-bit, day-by-day learnings that individually don't seem that significant or memorable, but that have no doubt provided me with a store of information I would not otherwise have, influenced my life, and provided part of the unseen base coat of the picture that is who I am. Reading has helped me learn to question, challenge, think, and purposefully consider what I believe. Reading books such as *The God Delusion* by atheist Richard Dawkins alongside *Bonhoeffer*, a biography of the famed Lutheran pastor, theologian, and anti-Nazi dissident—who was hanged because of his beliefs—have had the net effect of helping me think more deeply about my faith and strengthening it.

There is no single guidebook for listening to God and understanding discernment, but the combination of several works has helped illuminate my own journey toward some level of comprehension. I suspect a similar approach will help you as well. My starting point for learning more about spirituality or spiritual discernment has been the Bible. I confess that I have never been an avid Bible reader and still do not read it as much as I should. However, its truths have been a pervasive influence on my life, I continue to read it for guidance, and I'm convinced that reading it should be a starting point for listening to God about spirituality or spiritual discernment.

My reading over the years has been rather eclectic and not focused on spiritual matters, but most has been on fairly serious topics, including biographies of admirable people, that have significantly shaped my thinking. I read *The Aquarium Conspiracy: Personal and Social Transformation in the 1980s* shortly after its publication, and I have returned to it time and again over the years to help my thinking on paradigm shifts in our culture and in myself. I read *Embodying Forgiveness* by L. Gregory Jones several years ago and have continued to refer to it over the years. I never dreamed at the time that my reading *Man's Search for Meaning* by Viktor Frankl, *Discernment* by Henri Nouwen, and *Synchronicity* by Joseph Jaworski would influence my writing as they have in this book.

Reading typically means gathering information, acquiring new insights and knowledge, or mastering a new field, and many people read books or other types of material in seeking to discover God's guidance and way forward for them. Reading books by or about people who've faithfully lived a positive life can exercise a deep and positive influence on your life, like stepping out of this world and back into it again under the guidance of special men and women. Good books read with the right attitude can provide a language for understanding and describing your own identity, open your hearts to the signs of God's presence and direction, and help you discern His way forward for you.

The Book of Nature

Nouwen notes that nature points to God and offers signs and wonders indicating His presence and will, as "the sun and stars, plants and animals, and natural rhythms speak of God's glory, wonder, and ways."[6]

I make no claim to understanding how nature works and how the sun, stars, plants, and animals are so God-like in so many ways, but I do have a perspective that in several respects is unique. My first experience with the wonders of nature was long days driving a John Deere tractor on a farm in northeast Texas—feeling the cool breeze of the early spring air, smelling the soil turned in ribbons by the moldboard plow, eating a sack lunch in solitude under the stately pine and oak trees at the end of each row, hearing the chirp of crickets as night approached. The fresh air and beautiful surroundings experienced in solitude provided a sense of peace and relaxation, and a connection to nature that was as real as it is difficult to explain.

This exposure to nature while plowing a big tract of land fostered reflection, thought, prayer, and discernment. You're not really idle, but you're not active, either. You're alone, but not lonely. You experience solitude and nature, but not isolation. Solitude provides the opportunity to find communion with a God you can directly experience. Jesus is the best model for the value of solitude in nature. For example, Mark 1:12–13 tells us, "At once the Spirit sent him out into the wilderness, and he was in the wilderness forty days, being tempted by Satan. He was with the wild animals, and angels attended him."

Today we live in a busy, often hectic, world, where few people have an open field and a John Deere tractor to provide solitude. But silence and solitude in nature are available to you if you look for them. You can go for a run, take a long walk, enjoy a car ride, visit a park, or take advantage of many other opportunities to be alone without being lonely. You can be in solitude with yourself and nature and treat your situation as an opportunity to spend time in the presence of God and to listen to him.

Early in my work career, I worked full time with the Crow Indian Tribe, negotiating a coal lease agreement and managing initial mine construction activities on their reservation. The Crow Indian Reservation, home of approximately 7,000 tribal members, is located in southeastern Montana on semiarid, gently rolling land covered by prairie grasses, interspersed by hills, buttes, and wide river valleys, where the sky seems to always be clear and to have no limits. It's an enchanting land that beautifully showcases God's handy work. I spent a great deal of time there and came to love it. I held my first meeting with members of the tribe at the historic old Sheridan Inn just across the border in Sheridan, Wyoming. The tribal spokesman began the meeting by advising me, "The land is important to Indians. Whites do not understand this. To Indians, the land is the source of everything good. That steak, the salad, the glass, the tablecloth, the silver—all those come from the land. Strip mining coal must not destroy our land." So began my introduction to the book of nature through the eyes a group of Native Americans.

The fundamental idea embedded in Native American life is that the land is not just a means of survival or the setting for our affairs. It is a part of our being—our dynamic, significant, real self. Religion is understood as the relationship between living humans and other persons or things. These may include beings in the "natural world" of flora and fauna, and mountains, springs, lakes, and clouds. Native American spirituality suggests that the natural world is not just alive but has a spirit and is in fact an intricate web of life. The Native American spirituality teaches that every aspect of nature, from the soil that nourishes plants to the air we breathe, is sacred. This deep reverence for nature has allowed Native Americans to live in harmony with the earth for thousands of years and is something from which we all should take many lessons.

My wife Marcia and I have had opportunities to travel extensively and experience nature in its abundance and splendor. We have spent a great deal of time in the Rocky Mountains of Wyoming and Colorado and visited natural areas in several other countries, where we have experienced the beauty, mystery, and spirituality of nature's wonders.

Experiencing and being attuned to nature is a way of understanding the world that goes beyond the physical and material realm, and recognizes that humans are not separate from nature, but rather a part of it. Being attuned to nature goes beyond just admiring its beauty, to recognizing the spiritual essence within nature, spending time in it, and developing a relationship with it. This recognition of the interconnectedness between all living beings and the natural environment allows people to feel more grounded and connected to something larger than themselves and cultivate a deeper sense of meaning and purpose in their lives.

Prayer and contemplation can open your eyes to nature and how nature makes you more attentive to divine guidance, and serve as a living revelation of God's ways. It is not a possession to be conquered but a gift to be received with respect and gratitude—one that can give you a sense of peace and timelessness and remind you of the cycle of life and death we all go through.

The People You Meet

Nouwen says God speaks to people through those they meet in daily life, whether they are great in the eyes of the world or almost invisible in society. You can discern God's voice through others if you listen to wise counsel from friends, pastors, and those with professional expertise; people who can see through the fog that is created by your beliefs, wants, and longings and have their own ability to discern what is best for you and what is God's will.

God speaks through family members and close friends with whom you have a primary relationship—with whom there is a give and take and a willingness to forgive one another. Even if each of them cannot love you in every way you might like, or be everything you might prefer, each one can reflect an aspect of God's love, and when taken together they reflect the fullness of God in a way that is often missed in focusing on what each one has to offer.

My wife, Marcia, is number one on my list. Her love and commitment over the more than fifty years of our marriage has been a blessing from God. God also has spoken to me through many people I've encountered over the years. Three had a special effect. Neither of them was an "earth shaker," considered "great" in the eyes of the world, or an overtly religious or spiritual person, but each was a Christian and in combination they have been a mouthpiece for God and have taught me many of the things Jesus taught. First on the list is my dad, a "down-home" schoolteacher and farmer; no-nonsense, loving, supportive father, and, in the words of my brother, "the most honest man I ever knew." And J. Wayne Stark, a senior administrator at Texas A&M who frequently and consistently advised, "never, ever let anyone be nicer than you are," and walked his talk. And Jack Mahaffey, a boss who trusted me enough to let me do my job as I thought it needed to be done.

In addition to these, I have in my life many friends, neighbors, and community members who are living signs of God's love and direction in my life. Some are close friends and family who are not only enjoyable in the moment, but also a source of wonderful memories. Others are the "strangers" with whom I interact each day. They exhibit the signs of grace that seem to be God speaking through them.

Events

Nouwen wrote, "Certain events—current events, historical events, critical incidents and life circumstances—serve as signposts pointing to the will of God and the new creation for those with eyes to see and ears to hear."[7] Events are not just a series of happy or unhappy incidents, but are part of the shaping hands of God and continuing occasions to change your heart. Seemingly unrelated events in your life have brought you to where you are, and in every critical event, there's an opportunity for God to reveal a deeper truth than what you have seen in the past, as even small, insignificant events, ideas, and life circumstances can become occasions to discern aspects of God's will and calling in your life.

A good example in my life occurred on the first day of my two-year stint in the army. I happened to "sign in" at the officer orientation school at the same time as a large, heavyset, African American man, and we had a nice conversation. When classes started, I learned that this lieutenant had a PhD in sociology from a prominent Midwestern university, was active in the civil-rights movement, and was a really bright, thoughtful, engaging person. He finished first in our class. After the first week of the course, each Friday evening, he held court at a table in the corner of the officers' club dining room, led provocative, enlightening discussions, and shared his insider views on race relations, one of the great issues of our time. He began to open many of our eyes. He always invited me, and I benefitted immensely from the experience.

On another occasion a few years later, as I was walking down a sidewalk in Austin from my parked car to a hotel ballroom to attend a bar review class, I was confronted by a beggar asking for money. I turned him down, telling myself that as a poor law student I probably had no more money than he did.

Was God speaking to me through these events? I'm not sure, but I suspect He was. I do know that the army event was a lesson in the mistake of judging others on the basis of our prejudice or their skin color, or other such factors. I have since faced similar beggar situations on a number of occasions, and I recognize the controversial nature of giving money that can support the bad habits of street beggars, but fifty-odd years later I still wonder if God was speaking to me, and I gave the wrong answer.

There are no doubt other ways that people listen to God for guidance to overcome hardships and change their lives. A thought, a dream, an overheard conversation, quiet time with a good dog, or observing something that seems a little funny can help you relax and listen for help and may trigger ideas that lead to answers to difficult questions. Some people find that meditation is the answer. Regardless of what works for you, pay attention to your inner self. You may be near your answer, and all you need to do is to think about your situation to find the intuitive guidance that paves the way to the higher wisdom that will support and guide you.

Sometimes you will not receive clear guidance, and sometimes you will be disappointed by the results. Sometimes, you will make up your answers or just hear what you want to hear. When such things happen, you may wish to "double down" and use a more structured process of discernment to decide God's will.

QUESTIONS FOR REFLECTION

1. John Sage reached a point "where freedom and destiny merge." Describe a situation where you have reached that point.

2. What have been some events of synchronicity in your life? How have they affected you?
3. What do you believe is the origin of synchronicity?
4. Which of Nouwen's ways of listening to God works best for you?
5. Describe a meaningful "listening to God" experience you have had.

2
DISCERNING GOD'S WILL

And this is my prayer: that your love may abound more and more in knowledge and depth of insight, so that you may be able to discern what is best and may be pure and blameless for the day of Christ.
(Philippians 1:9–10)

As described in Chapter 1, Debbie Mosley believes she heard the word of God in the loud, clear voice from the back seat of her car on Highway 45. The rest of her story is as follows:

I was born in Fort Worth, Texas. My father was in the Air Force and my mother was a stay-at-home mom. Both of them had severe drinking problems and my father also had a gambling addiction. When my father had to be away from home, he would take me and my younger sister to my grandfather's house and my two brothers to my aunt's house. When I was six, my grandfather started sexually abusing both my sister and me. I don't have a whole lot of memories of anything in my childhood except the abuse. I do remember there were sometimes when my mom and my dad would get into fights—not physical, but yelling and screaming—and my dad would say things like, "Well, I'm gonna make sure that he doesn't do that to my babies again and I'm gonna go there and I'm gonna kill him." On one occasion he left and came back hours later. My sister and I thought the abuse would be over, but it wasn't. It didn't stop until my grandfather died when I was thirteen and my sister was eleven.

About that time my dad got out of the service, and we moved to New York, where he was raised. I just kind of rolled along. I don't have a lot of memories of things in my childhood. I think that's God's way of protecting me from the things that happened, because I don't have any happy memories of those times. When I was 14 or 15 my mom was still drinking, and my dad was out of the service and drinking more. I became a little promiscuous at my young age and started dabbling in drugs. At around age sixteen, my family came to Texas to visit my mom's sister. My cousin introduced me to this guy named John. We married when I was seventeen, moved from New York to Texas, and I had my first baby at eighteen. We were married for ten good years, until John had an affair with my best friend—who I had named my daughter, who died when ten days old, after. He divorced me and married her. Life went on for them and life stopped for me.

I really hit bottom. I started drinking, doing drugs, just being crazy. That lasted maybe a year and a half. I really didn't think I deserved to live because I was a failure at everything. I tried to kill myself a couple of times by taking too many pills and things like that or being very reckless with my life and doing whatever I wanted with whoever I wanted to.

I moved to Houston, but it wasn't any better here. I decided that I would kill myself— and really do it this time. That's when I started looking for a concrete pillar that I could crash my car into. I felt everybody would be relieved when I was gone because I was such a failure as a mother and daughter and everything. I was crying hysterically, but it was such a loud voice that I pulled the car over to the side of the road where I was going to kill myself and checked the back seat. Of course there was no one in the back seat. From that day forward my life changed.

I knew that was the Holy Spirit speaking very loudly and that I was worthy. During the chaos in my life I never could think straight. My brain didn't work that way. I didn't think about anything good. Everything was always bad but that voice turned me around and allowed me to move forward. I got counseling, got a job, and enjoyed a much better relationship with my babies—who were not babies at the time. Then I met my future husband when he was working as a supervisor where I got a job. He had the spirit that I was looking for and I set my sight on marrying him. We have had a great life together for thirty-eight years.

Debbie reconciled with her mother and with her encouragement started volunteering at The Bridge, an organization for abused women that provides services that include crisis intervention, emergency shelter, community education, on-site daycare, counseling, support groups, and parenting classes. She soon became its Executive Director, serving for thirty-six years until her recent retirement. She also volunteered as a Bridges To Life small-group facilitator for more than twenty years and worked forty, fourteen-week programs.

Unfortunately, whether decisions are big or small, people often stumble, engage in bad decision-making and behavior, and are "tossed back and forth by the waves, and blown here and there by every wind of teaching and by the cunning and craftiness of people in their deceitful scheming." (Ephesians 4:14) Debbie seems to have caught more than her share of the big waves, the high winds, and the bad people as she was growing up, and to pull herself out of it she needed to follow a process of discernment to help her address the difficulties and make the best decisions that reflected God's will.

Sometimes discernment involves truth and error, right and wrong, but it often boils down to deciding on the best between two valid options. To live a life of shalom you need to exercise discernment in every area of your life and exhibit a kind of wisdom that comes from insight as much as from learned experience and knowledge.

Discernment may seem like judgment, or being judgmental, but the difference is significant. We're surrounded by judgments, as our culture is strongly attached to categorizing and comparing; yet we're also told that it's not politically or even spiritually correct to judge, and we should endorse difference, see similarity, and accept that no one is better or worse than anyone else. Judgment is an opinion that implies a power differential: You perceive yourself to have power over another when you judge them.

Judgment assumes that the person judging has the power and right to determine what is good or bad in general, not just from their point of view.

Discernment, however, involves the cognitive ability of a person to distinguish what is appropriate or inappropriate—an ability that Debbie seemed totally devoid of in her youth, but one she demonstrated in spades during and after her recovery. With discernment you make good choices for yourself and for the good of others. It involves using perception, insight, and acumen to separate things mentally, recognize them as separate or different, and perceive them clearly. It helps you determine what is real and unreal, right and wrong, good and bad, effective and ineffective; and separate good from evil, truth from falsehood, wisdom from foolishness, and sometimes better from good. It's the ability to evaluate situations and choose courses of action while staying aware of the moral implication of all options.

Unfortunately, discernment is an area where many stumble. They exhibit little ability to measure the things they are taught against appropriate standards, and they unwittingly engage in bad decision-making and behavior. For example, Debbie's father's bad behavior made it difficult for her to distinguish between truth and error and left her subject to false teaching. False teaching then led to an unfruitful and disobedient living.

First Thessalonians 5:21–22 teaches that it is the responsibility of each of us to be discerning: "But examine everything carefully; hold fast to that which is good; abstain from every form of evil." The key to living an uncompromising life lies in your ability to exercise discernment in every area of your life. It is incumbent upon you to seize upon the discernment that God has provided for. Without it, you are at risk of being "tossed here and there by waves, and carried about by every wind of doctrine" (Ephesians 4:14). With it, you can make decisions that foster shalom.

How do you make tough choices? How do you weigh competing values? How do you discern the right path? Discerning the right choice is a little like taking a road trip. You have a mission, and you've got to determine how to get from point A to point B. While you don't have a physical resource for finding your way, you do have the gift of discernment: a collaboration of prayer, deliberation, and reason in which you determine God's will for your life.

St. Ignatius of Loyola offered guidelines for the discernment that will help you discover what God is calling you to do in the big and small decisions of your life, including decisions that will help you change your life and find shalom. St. Ignatius was born in the Basque country of northeastern Spain in 1491 and was raised to be a courtier and diplomat in service to the crown. He joined the army at seventeen, where he was said to be a fancy dresser, an expert dancer, and a womanizer who used his privileged status to escape prosecution for violent crimes he committed. He participated in many battles without injury, but in one a cannonball ricocheted off a nearby wall and fractured his right leg. In an era before anesthetics, he underwent several surgical operations to repair the leg, with his bones set and rebroken. In the end, the operations left his right leg shorter than the other. He limped for the rest of his life, with his military career over. While recovering from surgery, he spent hours dreaming. When he began to reflect on these dreams; he noticed that some thoughts left him sad while others made him happy, and little by little he came to perceive the different spirits that were moving him, which seems to be the beginning of his power of discernment, or decision-making. He realized God was affecting his feelings, and his feelings were drawing him toward an entirely new way of life.

After initial schooling in Barcelona, St. Ignatius spent much of his time engaging people in conversation about spiritual matters. Such conversations got him into trouble with the Spanish Inquisition and he was put in prison three times for interrogation. In one case he was held in custody for eighteen days without knowing the charges against him and in another one he was kept chained to a post in the middle of the building. The charge was always that he dared to speak of theological matters when he did not have a theology degree. Further, he was not ordained. In the end, he was always exonerated. In 1540, he and six companions founded the Society of Jesus, also known as the Jesuit Order or the Jesuits.

Ignatius recorded his thoughts in a journal, which ultimately became a series of spiritual exercises that have guided people for centuries in determining God's will and bringing shalom into their lives. We face many decisions in our lives: schooling, career, work, state of life, relationships, weighty commitments, as well as smaller decisions about our priorities and goals, how to spend our time, what to pay attention to and what to put off for another day. We have to make choices, weigh competing values, discern the right path. Ignatian spirituality gives us a practical way to approach such questions and discern God's will in our lives. St. Ignatius is considered one of the most important teachers of discernment. He put in writing his wisdom on discernment through *The Spiritual Exercises*, or what is called Ignatian Discernment. The following decision process is based on various online discussions of his Rules for Discernment of Spirits.

1. Identify the decision to be made or the issue to be resolved. The issue should be practical—about doing or not doing something—and an issue about which you have the right to make the decision. Discernment involves choosing between "goods" (such as between which school or church to attend) and not between good and evil. If your decision is between something good and something bad (such as cheating on a spouse), that's not a matter for discernment. You just need to do what you know is right.

2. Formulate two tentative responses to the issue. State the response as a choice between two specific, positive, concrete options. (What you will do, where, and when?) State the options in the way that your feelings initially seem to be drawing you.

3. Pray for guidance and openness to God's will, and for freedom from prejudgment and biases. Ask for that inner freedom and balance that allows you not to be inclined more toward one option than to the other. You may wish to discuss the matter with a mature person who can help you identify what obstacles you should pray about (such as inferiority complexes, superiority complexes, fears, greed, self-pity, envy, lust, desire for control, and so forth) that might limit your inner freedom and incline you to one alternative over the other.

4. Gather all the necessary information relating to the decision: Who? What? Where? When? How much? Why? Consult with everyone

who will be intimately affected by the decision being made: spouse, children, other family, friends, colleagues. Also, discuss this matter with someone who is not affected by the decision but is sensitive to the issue, such as a friend, counselor, priest, or minister who will be honest and objective with you.

5. List the advantages and disadvantages, reasons for and reasons against, each option. List all the reasons you can think of. Do not prejudge their merit, as you will evaluate them in the next step.

6. Do an evaluation of all the advantages and disadvantages, considering your needs, motives, and values. You may need to spend considerable time on this step. It may take weeks if you are making a major life decision. Asking four questions may be helpful.
    › Which advantages and disadvantages are the most important? Why?
    › What values are preserved or realized by each option? (Many advantages and disadvantages may be pointing to the same value.)
    › Which option more evidently leads to God's service and better serves the growth of your true self?
    › Which option seems more consistent with your own faith journey?

7. Observe the direction of your will while reflecting on the advantages and disadvantages. As you evaluate the choices, you may become more inclined toward one option and less inclined toward the other. These inclinations may fluctuate between options. Pay attention to these inner feelings. Pray for guidance about them. Eventually, your will is likely to focus on one of the alternatives. Christian choices are often beyond the merely rational or reasonable.

8. Trust in God and make your decision, even if you are not certain about it. Sometime a decision is unmistakably clear. You know what is right. If this is the case, proceed. In situations where the preferred

choice is not clear and you are presented with alternative courses of action that all seem attractive, you can discern the right choice by attending to the inner movements of your spirit. You can use your reason to weigh the matter carefully to attempt to come to a decision in line with your living out God's will in your life, considering which alternatives seem more reasonable and deciding according to the more weighty motives—not from your selfish inclinations. You can notice if any of the reasons listed stand out from the others and why and see which way this might point you.

9. Confirm the decision. Once you've considered the decision prayerfully, consulted others you trust, and have attained all the data you reasonably can, you need to take a leap of faith and make a decision.

10. Live with the decision for a while to see whether your thoughts, desires, and feelings continue to support it. The usual sign of this confirmation is an experience of peacefulness about the decision. The decision has a feeling of "rightness" about it, and you feel a sense of God's presence, blessing, and love. If not, new data is needed and the process should be redone.

You need to take time with discernment, be patient, trust the process, and ultimately trust that God will lead you to the right place, as He did with Debbie. In the end, if you do your part as best you can, follow what your heart and gut tell you to do and what seems right to you, you are likely to make decisions that are consistent with the will of God in your life and from which shalom will ensue. If there remains the question, "Is it God that is speaking or is it some other voice?" the surest sign that you know God's will in a certain decision you are contemplating is that you are left with peace and a sense of serenity with God. Even difficult decisions that will be hard to implement can give you peace when you have confidence it is God's will for you. This is a deep peace—not to be confused with a false peace that comes from glossing over differences and unresolved concerns, creating a superficial sense of harmony and well-being. It envisions a profound calm after all of the turbulence and turmoil associated with the situation has been confronted. Another sign to look for is events of synchronicity, when various things that occurred independently and at different times, and heretofore had not seemed to be related to one another, all of a sudden converge and fit together, or when the same message keeps coming through unrelated channels and in different ways; or all of a sudden something significant becomes clear in a vivid way.

If some aspect of what you are hearing seems incomplete or slightly off course, that means you need to take additional time and continue with the discernment. The process points the direction but does not provide a roadmap. To the extent that you continue to walk with God, you will keep moving in the right direction. As you cultivate a life of discernment, He continues to illuminate the path ahead, casting light on any missteps and revealing the way forward. You can never be certain that you are hearing God correctly. It is unlikely that all the signs will be present in any given circumstance. You interpret signals as ably as you can and move forward to act on what you believe God is asking of you, always listening and asking God to continue to guide you.

You also must love other people.

QUESTIONS FOR REFLECTION

1. Have you ever heard God like Debbie did?
2. What reading has helped you listen to God?
3. What person or persons have been most influential in your life?
4. What event has had the greatest effect on your life?
5. What has been your most difficult decision over the last several years?
6. Would a discernment process have been helpful in making that decision?

3

LOVING OTHERS

And now these three remain: faith, hope, and love.
But the greatest of these is love.
(1 Corinthians 13:13)

Most people today face personal problems, big and small, that are best addressed by acts of love. Many BTL participants have experienced situations where the depths of crime, depravity, and despair have led to the heights of love. Patricia Stonestreet and others have encountered both the lows and the highs, and their experiences provide guidance for anyone seeking to put such problems behind and move toward a life of shalom.

Early on a warm, muggy, June day in Houston, Patricia rang her daughter, Lisa, as usual—just to chat, as close friends do. Lisa didn't answer the phone. Patricia called time and again, but got no answer, as her feelings escalated from slight annoyance, through a dose of anxiety, to grave concern and fear. Anxious co-workers also tried to contact Lisa, with equal results and similar feelings.

Lisa, the youngest daughter of Patricia and her husband Lee, was twenty-eight years old, vibrant, full of vigor and hope: the essence of beauty and joy and the apple of her parents' eyes. She lived in an apartment in west Houston that Patricia, an interior decorator, had helped her decorate in a warm and welcoming décor that fit both their personalities. Later in the day, some of her co-workers found her dead in her bathtub.

Police determined that around 2:00 a.m. on the preceding night, a drug addict high on cocaine had broken into Lisa's apartment, brutally raped her several times, stabbed her in the eye, then strangled her and drowned her in her bathtub.

The devastation of this vicious murder left Patricia and her family and friends in tremendous turmoil—with gaping holes in their hearts as they continually asked the question, "Why?" The night after they buried Lisa, the family grieved together and, physically exhausted and emotionally spent, decided they would forgive Lisa's killer, at a time when they felt able to do so. At first their sadness, hurt, and anger won out. But over a period of nearly five years, Patricia became able to forgive her daughter's murderer.

While forgiveness helped the family cope with the tragedy, it did not remove the pain. Patricia watched her husband grieve himself to death. He died, Patricia believes, with, a broken heart, on Lisa's birthday one year before her killer was executed.

Patricia became a volunteer in the first Bridges To Life program, in 1999, and participated in a total of sixty-six programs—comprising more than 3,000 hours of volunteer time—in prisons throughout Texas, until her death of cancer in 2008. John Sage visited her in the hospital two days before her death and advised her that the BTL *Volunteer of the Year* award was being named after her in recognition of her demonstrated passion and commitment to the BTL mission and her obvious love of the unloved.

The list of BTL volunteers who have similarly gone beyond tragedy to love is a long one. Gay and John Van Osdall lost their daughter, Christine, to murder by a man she had dated, and they subsequently began volunteering with Bridges To Life, established a vibrant program with projects in three prisons in North Carolina, and Gay began her long-time service on the BTL board of directors. Judy Dunn's twelve-year-old daughter was murdered by her best friend, and Judy subsequently moved to Washington state, because of fear that the murderer would be released and come after her, and established Bridges To Life programs in six prisons there. Patricia, Judy, Gay, and John are the tip of the volunteer iceberg. To date 3,800 people have volunteered at Bridges To Life, and approximately 25 percent of them have been victims of serious crimes to themselves or their families. Thinking about their stories of evil and tragedy, then faith, hope, and love, will help you deal with less egregious, but nevertheless significant, personal problems that you may encounter.

Volunteering with Bridges To Life is not a comfortable assignment. You commit to two hours a week in prison for fourteen weeks. Prisons in Texas are usually not close to where you live, so you drive up to fifty miles or more, one way, to get there. You wait at the front gate and then go through a pat-down security check before being allowed to enter the prison. You feel the heebie-jeebies as you enter the lock-up and hear the clank of the heavy steel door behind you as you walk among a group of white-uniformed, elaborately tattooed people who you know have done bad stuff. Your unease gets worse when you see the sign explaining to the effect, "there will be no negotiating for hostage releases." You meet with your small group in a poorly ventilated, non-air-conditioned room on a hot night. You are put on hold until the "count" clears. After two hours, you wait in line to leave while the offenders are returned to their quarters. You drive home in the dark, ruminating on questions like: "How do people do things like they did?" "Why am I here?" "Am I really doing any good?"

You decide you are.

I think it has to do with love.

LOVE

Writer, literary scholar, and theologian C. S. Lewis (1898–1963) presented a model for love that is helpful in this situation. He wrote in *The Four Loves* that we experience love from two perspectives. People have their own desires and need for love from others (need love, such as the love that incarcerated people desire and need from others to motivate changes in their lives) and simple self-giving (gift-love, such as volunteers giving their time to visit prison inmates). Lewis also described four categories of love, based in part on the four Greek words for "love": affection, friendship, eros, and charity (agape).

- Affection is liking someone through the fondness of familiarity, such as family members or people who relate in familiar ways. It is present without coercion, and it does not require the recipient to have characteristics deemed "valuable" or worthy of love. An example is the love that Patricia, Gay, John, and Judy had for their daughters. Each of them was lovable, but their parents would have loved them regardless.

- Friendship is the strong and durable love between friends: the bond existing between people who share common values, interests, or activities. The classmates and co-workers of those who were murdered no doubt felt a strong friendship for those who were murdered and their families.

- Eros is the sense of "being in love" or "loving" someone from a romantic point of view.

- Charity, commonly called agape, or "God" love, is the highest, most pure form of love. It exists regardless of changing circumstances and is almost always used to describe the love that is of and from God. We are to love others with agape love, whether they deserve it or not.

The mindset behind agape love is selfless sacrificial service to others that accepts and embraces the wholeness of each person without reservation. The provider of agape love gives selflessly and intentionally for the best interests of the receiver without expecting anything in return. Agape love is the love that fuels BTL and motivates most of its volunteers. Volunteers—like Patricia, Judy, Gay, and John—helping incarcerated offenders are great examples of agape gift-love from which most people can learn.

Agape love is more an action than an emotion or feeling. It involves doing something for someone else with no expectation of anything in return from them. It's not "I want to do this for you so that I will feel good about myself," but instead is "I want to do this because you want or need it." Agape love is practiced with actions, not words. There is no set formula for what actions are best in all circumstances, but the following have worked well in demonstrating agape love among Bridges To Life volunteers and offenders, and should work equally well for anyone facing similar, bigger, or smaller such issues.

PRACTICING AGAPE LOVE

Practicing agape love is a challenging endeavor for several reasons. Agape love often requires you to extend grace and forgiveness in situations where it feels undeserved, to support others at the cost of your comfort, and to remain steadfast in love despite the lack of reciprocation. People frequently are prone to pride, jealousy, and impatience and often gravitate toward self-interest and self-preservation. Societal norms and the cultural emphasis on reciprocity can conflict with the principles of sacrificial, unconditional love. Therefore, practicing agape love calls for an intentional departure from the way society generally motivates people to act, and no set of actions applies in all cases. Introduced below are several actions that have worked in the BTL process and that can be considered on a case-by-case basis as you aim to demonstrate agape love when dealing with troublesome issues with other people.

Show Up

The late theoretical physicist, cosmologist, and author Stephen Hawking once said that showing up is half the battle. Filmmaker, actor, and comedian Woody Allen claimed it was more like 90 percent. Whatever the case, showing up is evidence that you care and is an element of agape love.

Showing up is a key aspect of BTL's prison programs and an incredibly powerful act of agape love in most situations. Many, if not most, offenders, and other people as well, have experienced lifetimes of disappointment and heartache when people who should have loved them (like parents or children) failed to show up for them. When volunteers show up and consistently do so for fourteen weeks in a BTL program, their presence is seen as a surprising act of love. John Romaka, introduced in Chapter 8, explained it this way: "I really liked the fact that people who . . . had no reason to care about me, came in on their own time and gave to me when I was not interested in myself."

Showing up is about appearing consistently for things that matter. This can be showing up at work, at the dinner table, at a scheduled meeting, for a group session, or for any of innumerable other commitments you have with someone else—and sometimes showing up by surprise. Being there for people is a starting point toward developing and maintaining good connections and relationships. By consistently turning up you stay connected, committed, and attuned, and demonstrate that you care enough, or love enough, to give your time to the other person.

Whether your relationships are strong or frayed, new or old, fleeting or long term, being there and being seen to be there nourishes and strengthens those connections. It shows respect for others, irrespective of their background, beliefs, or values, and is fundamental to agape love. It means acknowledging the inherent worth and dignity of every individual. In relationships with your friends, loved ones, and others, it's more important to be there for them—to show up—than to perform grand gestures. We all need to make showing up the attitude of our life.

Be Present

Showing up is being there physically, but you also need to be present—connect with the other person, listen with kindness, stay open-minded, avoid judgment. On the most basic level, being present means being focused on one thing—a person, a conversation, a project, a task in hand—without distraction, without wanting to be somewhere else, without being lost in thought. When you are present with other people, it means that you are giving them your full and conscious attention and awareness.

Being present with another is a form of unconditional love, because when you're truly present, there are no egos, judgments, agendas, or distractions involved; just one person being with another. Being fully present may well be the greatest gift you can give to another person.

In BTL small group sessions, it is important for group leaders to demonstrate their love by being present for group members. It's equally important for you to be present for people you love: connecting with your spouse rather than focusing on a TV show, listening empathetically to a child, putting the other person first in actions that may seem routine.

Following are some actions that can help you demonstrate your presence—and your love.

- Show up on time. Being late suggests that you don't care.
- Demonstrate your care and love by asking the other person about themselves and how they are doing.
- Get rid of all electronic devices except those specifically in use in your communication.
- Ask questions that indicate an interest in the other person and their views. Asking questions helps keep you present and mindful in a conversation. When you are asking questions, you are engaging with what the other person has to say, thinking about what else you would like to know, and trying to understand more about how they see the world.
- Listen with empathy.
- Be straightforward and honest, without judging the other person.

Listen

Most of us don't listen well. If you are not listening well, the message received can easily lead to confusion and prevent an accurate exchange of information and ideas. And perhaps more important, failing to listen effectively tells the speaker that you don't really care what they have to say, perhaps because you do not love them enough to care, and this ultimately can tend to hurt or even destroy your relationship. Over time, failing to listen and never really understanding others' needs or concerns sets the stage for continuing difficulties. On the other hand, putting aside what you're doing to really listen to someone—a friend, co-worker, spouse, child, or other acquaintance—is an act that demonstrates agape love. When you extend that type of generosity to your relationships—whether it's your friends, parents, siblings, or significant other—it can have a positive impact that extends well beyond you.

Listening is not a simple, passive task. It requires more than just being quiet and allowing someone to talk while you remain silent and appear to absorb information from them. Listening is an active process that involves hearing and understanding the words that are being spoken, but also observing the tone of voice, the volume, and other nonverbal signals such as facial expressions and body language. It also involves paying attention, thinking about what was said, and remembering the message. By striving to understand others' experiences, challenges, and emotions from their perspective, you can connect with them on a deeper level, embodying the essence of agape love.

Listening well is a learned skill that with effort can be developed over time. Observe someone who listens well and emulate them. Read a book on listening. Check online sources. Pursue some of the extensive available information for improving your listening skills.

Forgive

Forgiving people who have hurt you, even if you feel they don't deserve it, is another form of agape love. This is especially difficult if people do something horrible, such as what happened to Patricia, Judy, John, Gay, and so many BTL victim volunteers; and often is also hard to do in cases of small hurts and slights that occur on a day-to-day basis for all of us. If you are having difficulty in dealing with either type of situation, you need to pray for the grace to forgive and ask God for the agape love that forgives others. God's love in you will enable you to not hold grudges against those who hurt you. This does not mean overlooking a wrong, but it does mean choosing to release the offender from the debt to you.

Chapter 8 relates the story of how Judy Dunn learned about forgiveness in perhaps the hardest of all ways. Her thirteen-year-old daughter, Kelly, was brutally murdered by her twelve-year-old friend. Over a long period of time and through many struggles, Judy forgave him. All of us can learn a great deal from her experience that will help us in dealing with ours.

Show Love

Jesus teaches us to "love your neighbor as yourself" (Matthew 22:39). This extends beyond mere affection for those close to us, and encompasses kindness, compassion, and forgiveness to all people, regardless of their background or beliefs. If God's love is in your heart, you will love others, including those who seemingly don't deserve your love, especially those who have mistreated you or hurt you badly in one way or another. Agape love is unconditional, which means it does not depend on the other person's actions or responses. It is about loving others for who they are, rather than what they can give you or how they make you feel. This includes loving your enemies, praying for those who persecute you (Matthew 5:44), and unconditionally loving them by showing them the selfless and sacrificial love that God gives you. You love them the way they need to be loved, not the way you think they should be loved.

Think about Gay and John, as they sit in a small room deep in the bowels of the Craggy Prison near Asheville, North Carolina, meeting with a group of ten convicted felons. Most are probably locked up on drug, assault, or burglary charges, but one or two are likely in for murder. And one of them may have killed another family's daughter. Gay and John forgave the man who murdered Christine, but that did not take away the pain. It did, however, with God's grace, help them become loving spouses and loving parents to their son, and to love others as themselves. They developed empathy with offenders who have had very different perspectives and experiences in life than theirs. After mighty struggles, they are able to meet face to face with men who murdered others' loved ones, shake their hands, pray with them, listen to them, and give them their best. They do this routinely in prisons in North Carolina and Texas and demonstrate agape love. You can do the same for neighbors and enemies alike.

Serve Others

Agape love is not self-seeking. It seeks to serve others selflessly rather than to be served. It is willing to meet the needs of others without expecting anything in return—just as BTL volunteers know that the inmates they help will not be able to return the favor, and in most cases will never be seen again. When God's agape love is in your life, you will put the needs of others first rather than insisting that your own needs be met first.

Agape love is demonstrated through acts of service and sacrifice. We are called to humble ourselves and consider the needs of others above our own (Philippians 2:3-4). Jesus exemplified this when He washed the feet of His disciples, showing that true greatness comes from serving others (John 13:1-17).

The parable of the Good Samaritan in Luke 10:25–37 summarizes how we should love and treat our neighbors. In that parable, a man was beaten to near death and left for dead. A priest and a Levite passed by without helping the dying man. However, a Samaritan saw the helpless dying man, had compassion for him, and took care of him without expecting anything in return. This is what Christ expects us to do for others.

Here is a practical way to emulate the Good Samaritan's agape love:

- Look for opportunities to help those who are in need, whether it's a friend, a stranger, or someone in your community.
- Show kindness and compassion without expecting anything in return, just as the Good Samaritan did.
- Take the initiative to assist and support others, even if it requires going out of your way.

Being there for someone in their grief, partaking in acts of kindness and hospitality, and helping someone in need are all notable examples of service in agape love. Volunteer activities and community service projects also are great ways to practice agape love. Helping out at a local shelter or organizing a neighborhood cleanup can make a big difference. Simple acts like showing kindness to strangers, being there for someone during tough times without expecting anything in return, or supporting local causes can ripple through the community. Generosity, whether with your time, resources, or skills, is a clear demonstration of agape love.

Chapter 9 discusses other ways of demonstrating love through service.

THE PARADOX

Agape love has been presented earlier as serenity before God; sacrificial service to others, where you give selflessly and intentionally for the best interests of the receiver. You do something for someone else for their benefit, with no expectation of anything in return. Paradoxically, however, when you give agape love to another, you probably receive as much or more than they do, often in the form of one or more of the elements comprising shalom: absence of conflict, freedom from fear of violence, wholeness, completeness, health, welfare, safety, tranquility, contentment, soundness, prosperity, and rest.

This paradox is almost always experienced by BTL volunteers, who consistently see themselves benefiting more from their service than they give. One BTL victim volunteer, for example, reported that, "I was in a very dark place and didn't know how to come out of it. Learning to love others gave me my self-worth back and provided me a reason for being." Another said, "Love doesn't happen immediately. You come to understand life situations and other things, and your feelings become love." A third said participating in the program returned him from a life of despair to a life of wholeness and vitality. Such love not only benefited the recipients but also transformed the giver. Giving love can help transform you as well.

Agape love plays a vital role in personal relationships, such as those with family members, friends, co-workers, and partners. Practicing such love fosters a harmonious relationship with God and others that enables you to experience a sense of fulfillment and purpose. It aligns your actions with God's will, cultivating virtues such as humility, empathy, and resilience. This love prompts you to look beyond your immediate concerns, connect with others, and recognize the inherent worth and dignity of every individual.

Research shows that being kind and helping others improves mental health. We feel good when we can genuinely help someone else. That altruistic feeling shows up in many ways in our everyday lives. Agape love improves physical well-being because it eliminates much of the unneeded stress caused by repression and rigidity, and offers a connection that leads to a deep sense of acceptance, belonging, and personal growth and transformation. When you embody agape love in everyday actions, you help create a culture of care and responsibility that benefits everyone and can strengthen bonds and create a sense of trust and security.

It seems almost negligent or irreverent to write a chapter on love and not include the following verses from 1 Corinthians 13, beginning with verse 1:

If I speak in the tongues of men or of angels, but do not have love,
I am only a resounding gong or a clanging cymbal. If I have the gift

of prophecy and can fathom all mysteries and all knowledge, and if I have a faith that can move mountains, but do not have love, I am nothing. If I give all I possess to the poor and give over my body to hardship that I may boast, but do not have love, I gain nothing. Love is patient, love is kind. It does not envy, it does not boast, it is not proud. It does not dishonor others, it is not self-seeking, it is not easily angered, it keeps no record of wrongs. Love does not delight in evil but rejoices in the truth. It always protects, always trusts, always hopes, always perseveres. . . . And now these three remain: faith, hope and love. But the greatest of these is love.

I hope this chapter has suggested a reasonable application of these verses.

QUESTIONS FOR REFLECTION

1. Identify some examples of the four types of love in your life.
2. Which of the actions that demonstrate agape love is most important from your perspective?
3. What is the best way for you to serve others?
4. How has loving others benefited you?
5. What words in I Corinthians 13 are most meaningful to you?

4

LIVING YOUR FAITH

*Now faith is confidence in what we hope for and assurance
about what we do not see.* (*Hebrews 11:1*)

Charles Fisher's life demonstrates both the mystery and the power
of faith. He was born in 1967, in Oklahoma City, Oklahoma, the
fifth of seven children. When Charles was just over one and a half
years old, his dad was sent to jail. When he was released, he went out with
his buddies to drink beer and shoot pool. He was killed in a drunk driving
accident on the way home.

Charles's mother, Judy, was physically and mentally unable to handle
the stress of a house full of kids and a big extended family, so Charles and
his brother Kevin were placed in an orphanage. After being there about
three and a half years, they were adopted by their great uncle, Lester
Donald Fisher, and his wife Elizabeth. Lester, an electrical engineer who
worked for a big construction firm, bought a farm near a small town north
of Dallas. Charles grew up there milking cows, bailing hay, delivering
calves, and doing other farm work, along with his fair share of hunting,
fishing, and camping. He had a good relationship with his adopted parents.
Lester and Elizabeth didn't go to church but often took him to Sunday
school, dropped him off, and picked him up two hours later.

Charles's career as a troublemaker began at age fourteen, when he
and his brother drove their old 1967 pickup truck on a spree pulling down
rural mailboxes, just for the fun and excitement of it. A sheriff's deputy

saw them, picked them up, and took them to jail. Charles's parents got him released from jail—for the first time.

The family lived on the farm for about seven years and then moved to the Plano area, where Charles enrolled in Plano High School. In the ninth grade, he began playing football and drinking and socializing with team members. He was jailed twice for DWI and began smoking pot and using cocaine and other drugs. He was arrested for possession of a controlled substance and placed on probation. He violated his probation and was given a two-year prison sentence. He served twenty months behind bars.

Soon after Charles was released from prison, he met Anita, a five-foot-four brunette with long hair, brown eyes, fair complexion, and an aggressive personality She supported his need for another beer, another hit, or another dollar; and greased his slippery path into the druggy lifestyle. Charles says, "After a while, me and Anita were running the streets. Shooting cocaine and other stuff. My addiction got pretty bad." He ran with Anita through all his savings, was convicted again of possession of a controlled substance, and this time was sentenced to five years in prison.

Charles was released from prison after serving three years, and immediately returned to the streets, shooting cocaine, and living the life of a wild man addicted to drugs. His life continued snowballing down that very steep slope. He says, "Things that had not been normal became normal in my life."

Toward the end of a forty-day drug binge with Anita, Charles followed a man who was driving a Camaro Super Sport home from a car wash, pulled him out of the car, beat him up, took his wallet, cell phone, car, and car keys—and drove immediately to do more drugs and continue the party.

Three days later, Charles was "relaxing" in a motel room and Anita was out driving around in their new car when police arrested her. She ratted Charles out and told them where he was. They kicked the door in and arrested him. Charles was held in jail for twenty-two months, then tried and convicted of aggravated assault with a deadly weapon (a box cutter) and sentenced to twenty years in prison.

Charles was sent to the Coffield Prison, at that time one of the toughest, most violent prisons in the Texas system, to begin his third rodeo. He decided from the beginning that *if life's going to be violent, I will do the violence on others, rather than have the violence done to me.* He became a leader of a crime syndicate with members both inside and outside prisons. He looked the part: roughly six feet tall, 260 pounds (solid not fat), the obligatory tattoos, and an intensity that commanded prison "respect"—fear. After several years, Charles was assigned to work in the prison maintenance department handling work orders and other logistical matters, which positioned him to have the "inside scoop" and control the movement of contraband around the unit. He became "Big C" to prevent his real name from being known and was able to modify his tattoos and prevent prison officials from identifying him as a confirmed gang member. However, "Big C" participated in the normal gang mayhem and therefore had frequent run-ins with officers and several tours in ad seg (solitary confinement).

In ad seg, Charles was locked alone in a small cubicle the size of a tiny bathroom that rose to 130 degrees in the summer. He got out only thirty minutes a day, when officers chained him up, strip searched him, and allowed him to shower or participate in "recreation," but not both. He lived on baloney sandwiches from a "Johnny sack"—a small brown paper bag. Charles remembers a forty-five-day stretch that was almost intolerable: "I have dogs, and I wouldn't keep them in a cage that way."

Suffering has many faces: mental, physical, emotional, and spiritual, or often a combination of them. Suffering hurts. It isolates. It cripples. Suffering often knocks people to their knees, but it can also draw them closer to God. According to Charles, "Ad seg is usually one of two extremes. It makes suffering people become strong Christians, or it breaks them and makes them more angry. You can meet the most encouraging, strong Christian or the most evil man in ad seg, or in prison for that matter."

FIND YOUR FAITH

One cool October day an "I-60" (the form inmates use to request attendance at classes) "mysteriously" appeared on Charles's desk, requesting permission to attend a scheduled Kairos session. Not understanding where it had come from, he went to his supervisor, Mrs. Lumpkins, and asked her about it. Her response was clear and unequivocal: "Go to that class or you no longer work for me."

The Kairos Prison Ministry is a lay-led, interdenominational Christian ministry in which men and women volunteers bring Christ's love and forgiveness to prisoners and their families. Its programs include weekend experiences in prisons, followed by participants and guests gathering regularly for accountability, support, and prayer. Charles didn't want to attend, but he didn't want to give up the advantages of his job, so he very reluctantly followed Mrs. Lumpkins's "suggestion" and showed up at the Kairos gathering.

The night after his first session, he prayed a broken prayer: "God, don't be driving around north Texas saying you're here for me. If you are real, I want you to pull right down my street into my driveway, open my door, come into my living room, hit me in the chest, and say, 'Charles, I want you.'"

At next morning's session, a Kairos leader hung a large card with his real name on it around Charles's neck with a colorful ribbon, then hit him on the chest, and said, "Jesus loves you, and I'm here to show you that God has plans to prosper you and not to harm you."

That hit in the chest had a profound effect. Charles says, "Roughly two weeks later, I was laying in my bunk, thinking about that Kairos weekend. The Holy Spirit woke me up about three in the morning with words from Jeremiah 29:11–14. I first thought it was some prison gangster harassing me from over the wall. And I wasn't sure about looking at my Bible, as it was my prison phone book where I kept all my buddies' phone numbers—so when I got out, I could contact them, continue my life of crime, and become a better criminal."

God prevailed. Charles pulled out the Bible and read from Jeremiah.

For I know the plans I have for you," declares the LORD, "plans to prosper you and not to harm you, plans to give you hope and a future. Then you will call on me and come and pray to me, and I will listen to you. You will seek me and find me when you seek me with all your heart. I will be found by you," declares the LORD, "and will bring you back from captivity. I will gather you from all the nations and places where I have banished you," declares the LORD, "and will bring you back to the place from which I carried you into exile."

Charles had not been to church since he was a kid, didn't go to chapel, and certainly didn't know Christ. It seemed to him that the love of the volunteers (who he recognized had left their jobs, homes, and families to visit inmates in their dark hours) was his first time to experience the love of Christ. He says: "The Kairos experience was the first time I ever really felt God wanted a relationship with me. I believed in God but I didn't know Jesus. Suffering brought that about. My suffering helped me picture Christ's journey to the cross."

Charles felt he was in a hopeless situation. He saw all the razor wire, the concrete, the bricks, the isolation cells, the 130-degree summer heat, the predictable prison mayhem. He had not behaved and had been in ad seg for bad behavior too many times to count. He was looking at twenty years, at the least, and maybe life in prison.

Charles started attending monthly Kairos retreats and thinking more about his future. He came to see that broken prayer during the Kairos Ministry weekend as the first time God had spoken to him. Charles says, "He wanted a relationship with me. God showed me Jesus on the cross. I've seen Jesus on the cross and I've seen suffering. My suffering was so minimal in comparison."

Charles continues, "Shortly after that, I encountered Jesus through a vision of His journey to the cross. I suddenly found myself in a dirty, dusty street in Jerusalem as the crowds are shouting 'Crucify Him!' I became a Roman soldier who was beating and whipping Jesus on the back and humiliating him before the frenzied crowd. I finally became the soldier who nailed him to the cross! This spiritual experience wrecked me. There wasn't any reason I had the vision, but the clarity and dirtiness of it has never left my soul. I began to change. I learned to read the Bible and memorize scripture. I started listening to Adrian Rogers sermons on the Radio instead of AC/DC music. I got up early and prayed in silence before the prison got loud and chaotic. I began to be at peace with all men where it was within my power to do so. I no longer wanted to hit people in their mouth, I no longer wanted to do drugs, and especially no longer wanted to be part of a gang."

Charles relates that one night the Holy Spirit told him he should "go down and talk to the prison chaplain and tell him you're going to be his clerk." He did, explained his full story, and also told him how he had changed his life. The chaplain started laughing. Charles was embarrassed and turned to leave. The chaplain said, "Fisher, you start tomorrow at 3:30."

Charles explained an important part of this job: "I became the eyes and ears of the chaplain. Not a snitch, because the chaplain gave me the authority, and God gave him the authority. I considered this my first test from God—to use his authority correctly."

The chaplain signed Charles up for a slate of classes including Bridges To Life, which Charles knew nothing about. He says, "The BTL experience caused me to vow that I would never drink and drive again, helped me develop empathy for victims and more respect for women, made me feel part of something bigger than myself, and changed the trajectory of my life."

On Charles's forty-first birthday, his birth mom, Judy, came back into his life. He was blown away to learn that at the same time of his experience attending the Kairos program and accepting Christ, his mom attended a little church out in the country in Oklahoma and became a Christian. They began to grow in their faith together and developed a great relationship.

Charles came up for parole consideration in 2010. He started fasting and praying, "God, I don't know what my future looks like. I'm not sitting here praying for you to put me out of prison. But if You open the door, I will go back in as a minister to help others get out of prison."

Charles was granted parole and released from prison within a year, after a total of twelve and a half years of incarceration. He reflects on prison as a classroom and the world as his teacher and says, "My stepfather used to tell me to learn something new every day. I asked him once, 'what happens if I don't learn something every day?' He laughed, looked me in the eyes, and said, 'boy you'll never be that smart.' I didn't know whether it was an insult or a gift. But today, I realize he was advising me to learn from the adversity in my life."

LIVE YOUR FAITH

Ten years after attending his first Kairos event, Charles returned to prison as a Kairos volunteer minister to share his life and experiences with others. He also got involved in the Bill Glass prison ministry, founded by the former football star, and known for its high-energy Day of Champions and Weekend of Champions events conducted inside prisons across the country. On one occasion, Charles was attending an event with an evening orientation session in Huntsville and a visit the following morning to the Eastham prison unit in Lovelady, around thirty miles away. He needed a ride to the unit, so the orientation leader asked the group of over fifty volunteers if someone would give him a ride the following morning. No one wanted to take this big, burly, tattooed, scary looking ex-con on a pre-dawn ride down the desolate, narrow, tree-bordered black top roads to Lovelady. Finally, after a long pause, Jim Buffington reluctantly agreed. During the drive Jim tried to fake interest with a conversation. He asked, "So—Charles, how did you get involved in prison ministry?"

Charles responded, "Well—I was in prison for aggravated robbery with a deadly weapon. Incarcerated on a twenty-year sentence."

Jim's jaw hit the floor. Then he told Charles his story of how he and his family were victims of crime, as his father had hired a man to kill his mother.

Charles continued, "When I was in prison, I took a program called Bridges To Life. It changed my life."

Jim's jaw almost fell through the floor this time. Jim explained that he had recently been hired as the chief operating officer of BTL—and that one of his first tasks was to find a graduate who had been released from prison to speak at the organization's fundraising luncheon that was scheduled soon in Arlington. After some discussion, Charles agreed to speak. In the process, he told Jim that if he ever needed a staff member for BTL, he would like to be considered.

Charles's story has an epilogue.

Charles met Nicole, and they married soon thereafter. He prayed for her before he met her. He believes God chose her specifically for him, and He has taken the two of them and made them into one flesh.

Years after he found the mystery I-60 and was pressured into attending the Kairos weekend, one of his former "enemies"—an inmate whom Charles had been harassing, intimidating, and extorting—approached Charles at a Kairos meeting and told him he had put the I-60 in for him to go to the session. The man said, "When I put you up for the class, I never thought you would change this much."

Also years later, Charles saw the chaplain who had laughed before offering him the job as his clerk and asked him why he had laughed at him. The chaplain answered, "Fisher, don't you realize I had been praying for a new clerk. No sooner than I had said 'amen,' you walked in my door. I was laughing at God, not at you." Charles says, "Learning why the chaplain was laughing changed my whole perspective from being embarrassed to being proud to be a Christian."

Soon after he met Jim Buffington, Charles started volunteering with BTL and Jim offered him a full-time job as a Regional Coordinator for the Dallas/Fort Worth region. Charles says, "I had been praying and fasting for eleven months on my desire to get into prison ministry. I felt like I had won the spiritual lottery. It was a divine moment."

Charles's faith is the foundation of his life, like the rock on which a wise man built his house in Matthew 7:24. He says, "I used to be miserable and see the world as a place of desperation and despair. I've now changed my perspective, and God has shown me there are good people in the world. I have been able to think of others and help them through their difficulties, just as God showed me a way through mine. I knew I was called to be a minister the first time I was able to go back to the Coffield Unit, where I spent ten and a half years, and preach a sermon. For me, faith requires trust. I cannot walk by faith if I don't trust the Lord. I wake every morning by asking the question: Do I trust Him? I answer 'yes' almost every time. I am fallible and not always sinless, but when I do fail, I confess and repent and try to continue to abide in the way. I strengthen my faith by believing in the joy of the Lord and that apart from Him I can do nothing. And I try to help others see a picture of faith that will help them activate their own faith, because most people want to see a sermon, not just hear a sermon."

God met Charles where he was, and he experienced a positive faith journey. His faith didn't provide Charles a guarantee of success or a certainty that his life would be better. It didn't promise that he would avoid ad seg or get his parole approved. But it did give him hope for something better: not just a wish, and not quite a belief, but a heartfelt confidence that he could improve his life and a reason for doing so. His motivation turned from simply avoiding the cops and staying out of prison, to becoming God's man and identifying himself with God. Faith brought Charles a sense of purpose, belonging, and hope, while also providing a moral compass and a source of comfort during difficult times. It helped him find good in a world of brutality, ugliness, and injustice. It fostered confidence, discernment, and peace; and it helped him view his life through a different lens, put his trust in God, and live a life of shalom.

Faith can do the same for you.

James 2:26 states, "For as the body without the spirit is dead, so faith without works is dead also." Faith is an expression of hope that goes beyond the conscious mind and influences your actions. It shapes every aspect of your life: your purpose, your thoughts, your decisions, your relationships, your ability to identify and use your talents, and how you handle your challenges as well as your successes. You demonstrate your faith in God by what you do and how you live.

Father Bernard Häring, moral theologian and Catholic priest, wrote in *Hope is the Remedy* that hope goes beyond the conscious mind and influences your actions. Faith is a theological virtue by which we believe in God and believe all that he has said and revealed to us. Biblical hope is built on faith. Hope is the earnest anticipation that comes with believing something good—a confident expectation that naturally stems from faith; a peaceful assurance that something that hasn't happened yet will indeed happen.

Think of faith and hope each as an oar in your rowboat of life. They work together to move you forward. When everything seems unsure, and you don't know what's coming, faith stops you from giving up and helps you stay positive about the future. It helps you pray rather than worry, overcome your fears, handle your mistakes, improve your relationships, deal with your anger. It allows you to "let go and let God," and is a compass that keeps you centered with the hope that things will work out and the realization that you are not alone and can trust God to help you live a life of shalom.

Charles is often referred to as the "velvet hammer" because of his soft love for God and the inmates he's working with, and his hard insistence that offenders do the right thing. The BTL Regional Coordinator job justified Charles's faith, fulfilled his hope, and provided an opportunity for him to act. Chapter 5 will discuss hope from the viewpoint of someone, like many of us, who is still struggling with the concept.

QUESTIONS FOR REFLECTION

1. What do you think are the key events in Charles's faith journey?
2. Did any cases of synchronicity play a role in Charles's faith?
3. Has any such event occurred in your life? Discuss.
4. How did faith affect Charles's life?
5. Do you believe faith or hope comes first?

5

CULTIVATING HOPE

*Not only so, but we also glory in our sufferings, because we know
that suffering produces perseverance; perseverance, character;
and character, hope.* (Romans 5:3–4)

Albert Einstein said, "Learn from yesterday, live for today, hope for tomorrow." Eddie Gaston has experienced all three: dreams and hopes, disappointments and setbacks, learnings, the return of hope, more setbacks, and continuing hope. He struggles with hope, and we can learn from his struggles.

Hope is our quiet, never-ending dream for the future; a feeling of expectation, a desire or wish for a certain thing to happen. Some say it's the belief that good things are ahead. The Bible speaks of hope in God. "May the God of hope fill you with all joy and peace as you trust in him, so that you may overflow with hope by the power of the Holy Spirit" (Romans 15:13).

Biblical hope has as its foundation faith in God and is a certain expectation that God will do what he has said. Hebrews 11:1 says, "Now faith is confidence in what we hope for and assurance about what we do not see."

With faith you actually believe there is a power in the universe which is God. Faith helps you see God working in your past, see meaning in many events of synchronicity, see your life as it is, and believe that He will work in your life in the future. Biblical hope is a consequence of faith regarding the future. Hope is humbler than faith, since no one can know the future, and the word "hope" conveys doubt. You can believe something will happen, but you can't know it will. You can learn from your past and live in the present, but you can only hope for the future.

In February 1968, just two months before he was assassinated, Martin Luther King, Jr. said in a Washington, D.C. address: "We must accept finite disappointment, but never lose infinite hope."

I take his words to mean that he believed you can always hope. You may have challenges and setbacks that put you in danger of giving up on your goals, dreams, and hopes, but they should never prevent you from imagining a better, more just, future or a life of shalom. Sometimes you have to accept disappointment, but you should always remember that there is an infinite reservoir of hope available. Accepting that setbacks are a normal part of life and that hope has no limits frees you to view and deal with your disappointments and failures as something you can always conquer. This belief feeds Eddie's struggles as he continues to hope.

BUILD HOPE

Eddie Gaston was born in Butzbach, Germany, where he was adopted, the youngest of three brothers. His family moved to Texas when he was two years old. His adoptive mother was diagnosed with a serious illness when he was eleven. He reflects that as he watched her decline, what he had been calling faith was really his wishing and hoping for the best. It was plain to see that his mom was getting worse. Eddie tried to maintain faith that she would get better, but the sickness decimated both her body and his faith.

Eddie's mom died when he was thirteen. Most of the kids in his class came to her funeral. Eddie hated their "normal" lives, or perhaps actually resented his lack of one. The presence of the kids he was close to was comforting, but the attention of those he wasn't close to angered him. Their condolences fell flat. He hated that they were so close to his pain and tragedy but weren't feeling it. His hope that his mother would get better was replaced by a hopeless feeling about his future. A void in his heart was filled with anger toward God.

After understandable struggles, Eddie pulled his life together, graduated from high school, and had hopes for his future. Then when he was twenty-nine years old, Eddie and a man had a fight. It went terribly wrong, and the man died. Eddie didn't intend to kill him and was remorseful for what he did, but a jury found him guilty of murder and he was sentenced to fifty years in prison, with a requirement to serve half the sentence before being eligible for parole. He thought there was no way he could do that kind of time, or survive, or continue living. He describes the futility he felt with a joke he had heard in the county jail: "A defendant stands before the judge. The robed figure looks down and says, 'you've been found guilty, and the jury has sentenced you to fifty years.' The perpetrator says, 'B-b-but judge, I can't do fifty years.' The judge replies, 'Oh, that's all right. Just go down there and do as much as you can.'"

Eddie entered the hopelessness of a prison cell and, again, lost all hope for his life. He says, "When I first got there, I believed in God, but I had no connection with Him. Prison was vicious—a scary and rough situation—and I didn't understand how He would carry me. I saw no light at the end of the tunnel."

Time heals many wounds and sometimes helps despair evolve to hope. And it did for Eddie. He says, "I attended some church services in prison which gave me hope in Jesus Christ. I spoke to some old school residents—guys who had from fifteen to twenty years prison time behind them—whose strength inspired me. I enrolled in some faith-based programs, including Bridges To Life, and college classes. It all gave me purpose and hope for a better future. My pity-party, woe-is-me attitude changed to where I decided I was going to make the best of my situation." He continues, "Over time, I read the Bible and prayed for a real connection with God. Gradually, I calmed down, more honestly assessed my life, and learned not to worry about what I could not control. I memorized the Serenity Prayer and said it daily to center and ground me for another trying day of prison."

God grant me the serenity
to accept the things I cannot change;
courage to change the things I can;
and wisdom to know the difference.
Living one day at a time;
enjoying one moment at a time;

accepting hardships as the pathway to peace;
taking, as He did, this sinful world
as it is, not as I would have it;
trusting that He will make all things right
if I surrender to His Will;
that I may be reasonably happy in this life
and supremely happy with Him
forever in the next.
Amen.

God carried Eddie through, and this gave him hope. While in prison, he earned three college degrees, including a BBA in management from Texas A&M Central Texas—Summa Cum Laude. He organized numerous Bible studies on different cell blocks, wrote numerous short stories and five novels, and never received a major disciplinary case.

Eddie was paroled after twenty-five years in prison, the first time he was eligible for consideration. Upon release, he was deported back to Germany and escorted from the plane into the Frankfurt Airport where ICE agents wished him luck and left him standing in the terminal, fresh out of prison and homeless. He had never used a cell phone or the internet, he didn't speak German, and he had no family or friends living in Germany. Eddie made his way to a homeless shelter and filed paperwork to get his German ID and start a life as a German citizen who had spent fifty of his fifty-four years in the US.

He began working as a caretaker/janitor at a church, where he has been employed for over two years. He earned a personal fitness trainer certification and began work on building a client list. His novel, *His Amazing Grace*, was published. Eddie has done and is doing the best he can. He says:

I see that part of my struggle is sometimes hoping for too much and in so doing, I take present blessings for granted. The Serenity Prayer speaks of being "reasonably happy" in this life. I sometimes forget all the blessings that are more than enough to make me reasonably happy. As I hope and wish for more, I sometimes forget the blessings of the past and present. And when the blessings I'm hoping for don't come, I can begin to feel a little hopeless. It's kind of like the windshield and the rearview mirror in a car. A good driver can't spend all of his time looking through either one. The windshield is bigger and deserves most of the driver's focus. The rearview mirror is much smaller, but still needs to be referenced periodically. The good driver sits between the hope of a wide-open future, and the reflections of past struggles and blessings. I not only hope for, but also work toward, a better job, nicer apartment, and financial security. Setbacks sadden me and sometimes cause my hope to falter. In those moments, I reflect on my time in prison. I remember thinking about when—if ever—I would be able to go outside when I wanted, breathe fresh, free-world air. Sit on a bench with no oversight, not having chain-link fences and razor wire obscuring my view. Being able to eat my choice of food. Drink a good, quality cup of coffee. See friends. Make new ones. Be with family. All the things I can do now. And so I am blessed to say I am reasonably happy. And still hopeful for the future.

Maintain Hope

When you focus on the future, you do one of three things:

- You wish or fantasize, which involves big dreams that are mostly for fun or entertainment.
- You dwell, which involves focusing on all the bad stuff that might or might not happen.
- You hope, which involves envisioning the future and recognizing the inevitability of challenges, as well as the expectation of positive events.

Which of the three describe Eddie? When he was in prison, did he wish for or fantasize about the successes he would have upon release? Is he dwelling on his current situation, his mind making it worse than it is? Will he be able to maintain hope even in the face of difficulties? Will his hope propel him to actions and lead to positive events?

Wishing, fantasizing, or dwelling all involve a person thinking about a better future, believing that the odds are in their favor, and somehow through their actions or luck or perhaps divine intervention believing their future will be bright. Hope is different. It leads to future success in a way that wishful thinking or dwelling on an issue does not. Hopeful people know the odds are against them. They persist anyway and make no claims about the future, but believe that hope requires acting toward the hoped-for goal. A story of two women demonstrates the concept. One is continually abused by her common law husband, and the other has been diagnosed with cancer. The first says, "I hope my husband doesn't beat me anymore," and continues to live with her situation. The second says, "I hope to beat this cancer," and follows the best medical advice available. Which has true hope? The one who is being abused has only a wish. She has no real faith and is doing nothing to help God work in her life. The woman with cancer prays to God and seeks medical help. She has hope.

You don't have faith or hope for their own sake. There is no value in that. What matters is the object of your faith and hope—what you believe in and expect. Hope caused many who have gone before us to sacrifice, give, serve, even lose their lives. People pray, work, and endure hardship, trials, and struggles because of hope for solutions to problems or for things they want. If you remove hope then you will discover that your joy, enthusiasm, peace, focus, motivation, and other things attached to life will be diminished.

Hope is not just a way of avoiding problems, but is a motivation to help you keep going in the face of adversity. Hope requires you to take actions and work hard to make what you want to happen actually happen. You won't act unless you hope your action is going to do some good, so you need to hope to get you going. When action generates successes, that leads to more hope. It's circular. And conversely, if despair and hopelessness get you down and you don't do anything, you become more hopeless.

We all have problems and unmet needs, and no one is immune from life's challenges. There are many ways to help you keep up hope in stressful and overwhelming situations. Some things you can do include the following:

- You can pray. When you pray to God you open your mind to Him and ask for help. In doing so, you acknowledge your weaknesses and accept that you are not all-powerful and that you need help from God. You construct a mental image of what hope really is. You acknowledge His power and your belief that addressing your situation is possible. When you do this, you believe more strongly and work harder and more intelligently, often in many small ways, to do your part in making your hopes a reality.

- You can acknowledge the reality that there's always hope, no matter how difficult or dire a situation may seem. Thoughts and feelings connected to hopelessness are almost always tied to a negative prediction about the future—even when the facts don't warrant such a conclusion—and to being convinced that this prediction is an established fact. Think of Eddie's ups and downs: the feelings of hope as he anticipated release from prison, followed by the hopelessness he sometimes felt in adjusting to life in the free world, his sense of hopelessness being reversed by even one event of good fortune, and then returning when problems developed.

- You can find inspirational media (such as a good book or favorite podcast) and "mentors" (such as a friend or pastor) to turn to. Building a hopeful mindset involves teamwork, sharing your goals, successes, and setbacks with a support network of people who care about you.

- You can exhibit acts of kindness. If you see someone struggling under a heavy load, offer a hand. Donate unwanted clothes to a charity. Help someone lost with directions. Give a thoughtful gift. Offer your help. Think about where your skills lie, and then ask the person what they need. Treat others the way they want to be treated. Do your best to follow the "golden rule." Paradoxically, helping others is often the best way to help yourself.

- You can cultivate more positive feelings through good habits such as having a positive morning routine, eating healthy food, getting regular exercise, playing a musical instrument, and spending time with friends. Positive feelings foster hope.

- You can maintain a grateful heart. A feeling of gratitude in response to God's grace and to others who help you plays a key role in building and maintaining relationships that foster hope. Hope helps you get through difficult times and flourish in good times, and contributes to your overall sense of well-being and happiness that then circles back to increase your hope. Giving thanks to God helps you have a closer connection with Him, trust in Him, believe He will take care of you, and not be so proud that you try to do everything on your own. Your focus on what you have instead of what you don't have gives you hope. Spending a few minutes each day recounting the positives in one's life—even small ones like noticing a moment of calm in the sunshine, or the "high" of a brisk run around your neighborhood—can have enormous impact.

- You can set goals, discussed in more detail in Chapter 11. Science has identified four components of goals that are essential for any lasting sense of hope: realistic goals to pursue, pathways to achieve the goals, the confidence that you can achieve them, and the support to help overcome adversity along the way. Accomplishing the goals is a success that provides the optimism that leads to hope.

Hope can be an opportunity for you to process events that seem insurmountable, helping you see a pathway from one stage of life to the next and decide to take actions that are appropriate. Buddhist peace activist Daisaku Ikeda has written: "When we change our inner determination, everything begins to move in a new direction. The moment we make a powerful resolve, every nerve and fiber in our being will immediately orient itself toward the fulfillment of this goal or desire. On the other hand, if we think, "This is never going to work out," then every cell in our body will be deflated and give up the fight. Hope, in this sense, is a decision."[8]

For hope to be real and attainable, you need a powerful resolve to pull you in the direction of fulfilling your goal or desire. You need a purpose in your life—the subject of discussion in the next chapter.

QUESTIONS FOR REFLECTION

1. How do you describe the difference between faith and hope?
2. How do you describe the difference between a wish and hope?
3. What takes your hope away?
4. What gives you hope?
5. Why is hope important to you?

6

LIVING FOR A PURPOSE

And we know that in all things God works for the good of those who love him,
who have been called according to his purpose. (Romans 8:28)

After the great fire of 1666 destroyed London, the famous architect, Christopher Wren, was commissioned to rebuild St. Paul's Cathedral. He is said to have observed three bricklayers on a scaffold, one crouched, one half-standing and one standing tall, working very hard and fast. Wren asked the first man what he was doing, to which the bricklayer replied, "I'm a bricklayer. I'm working hard laying bricks to feed my family." The second bricklayer responded, "I'm a builder. I'm building a wall." The third brick layer, when asked the same question, replied, "I'm a cathedral builder. I'm building a great cathedral to The Almighty." Three people were working on the same wall, doing the same work, but with totally different perspectives and objectives. The "cathedral builder" demonstrated a personal expression of purpose that gave a higher meaning to his work and life.

Happiness is rarely a good enough reason to do anything, while purpose is an engine that motivates a meaningful life. Your life purpose consists of your central motivating aims—to lay bricks or to build a cathedral, or whatever other reasons you get up in the morning. It defines what you do and don't do; provides a foundation for making decisions, allocating time, and using resources; dictates your goals; and focuses your being by concentrating your effort and energy toward things that are greater than yourself. It demonstrates who you really are and answers the "headstone" question—*What do I want my epitaph to be or what do I want people to say at my memorial service?*

Victor Frankl's classic book, *Man's Search for Meaning*, speaks to the value of purpose. Frankl (1905–1997) was an Austrian psychiatrist and psychotherapist who personally witnessed and experienced daily acts of extreme antisemitism and persecution. He experienced the loss of his parents and wife, and endured personal physical abuse, malnutrition, emotional humiliation, and torture in four different Nazi concentration camps. His experience of finding meaning in life during the time he was incarcerated molded his philosophy that the search for meaning is the drive behind human behavior. He observed that those who had a purpose or reason to continue to live that was beyond themselves tended to survive the holocaust, while those who were focused primarily on themselves did not. He was fond of quoting Friedrich Nietzsche, "He who has a why to live can bear with almost any how."[9]

Frankl wrote that there is no single meaning of life, purpose is unique for everyone, and each person can discover something that gives life purpose. For some people, it is connected to meaningful, satisfying work. For others, purpose lies in their responsibilities to their family or friends. Others seek meaning through spirituality or religious beliefs. However, like success and happiness, purpose cannot be effectively pursued for its own sake. He wrote:

> Don't aim at success—the more you aim at it and make it a target, the more you are going to miss it. For success, like happiness, cannot be pursued; it must ensue, and it only does so as the unintended side-effect of one's personal dedication to a cause greater than oneself or as the by-product of one's surrender to a person other than one's self. Happiness must happen, and the same holds for success. You have to let it happen by not caring about it.[10]

Although Frankl "just let it happen," researchers have identified several consistent strategies that helped him deal with the pain and suffering in the camps, and brought purpose to his life in the chaotic environment in which he lived. Applying similar strategies, as discussed below, will in most cases have the side effect of helping purpose to ensue in your life.

SERVE OTHERS

Frankl found that serving people helped him change his focus from himself to others, transcend his suffering, and live a life of purpose within an environment that was designed to take it away. In the camps he gave public talks on different topics relating to medicine and psychology, organized and was in charge of a team that ran suicide prevention programs, and helped depressed and suicidal prisoners find reasons to live. He was once asked if he wanted to work as a doctor in another camp. He was skeptical of the offer, concerned that it was a trick to get him into a death camp. However, he decided to go, as he felt that if he spent the last remaining months of his life caring for sick prisoners, at least his suffering and death would have some meaning.

Frankl wrote, "The more one forgets himself—by giving himself to a cause to serve or another person to love—the more human he is and the more he actualizes himself."[11]

John Romaka, whose story is told in Chapter 9, struggled with alcohol and drugs, checked into the Houston Salvation Army Adult Rehabilitation Center (ARC) to dry out, became its Operations Manager, and subsequently was promoted to a senior position in the city-wide organization. He talks about the problems of focusing on self and how serving others has given purpose to his life:

Service keeps me sober. Drugs and alcohol were never my problem. My problem was an obsession with self: adhering to my selfish thoughts and wants, wanting what I wanted when I wanted it, and not caring about the consequences. Working at the Center allowed me to pour my life and experiences into guys who have gone through hell on earth, and now are at the right place at the right time. One of the big differences between my previous jobs and the one at the ARC is that I found my purpose in serving others. My purpose in previous jobs included leading people in their retirement planning, taking care of their families, and having a good life. I was good at that and a lot of good came from it. They were good paying jobs that provided a level of satisfaction but not the intimacy that goes with truly serving others. In the ARC job, I got to see miracles happen every day. I saw men who were broken be restored. Men who were bad fathers become great fathers. Broken families come together. Guys given their lives back. And I was part of that, serving them at a very personal level. I learned that nothing gives my life more meaning than helping change someone's life, and the way to do that is to serve them.

You, like most people, probably possess an intrinsic desire to help others. Doing so underscores your interconnectedness and empathy, makes you feel good about yourself, and helps you feel like you are a good person making a difference in the world. And in one of life's real paradoxes, the more you serve others, the more you help yourself and bring purpose to your life.

COMMIT TO YOUR DECISIONS

Commitment is the act of dedicating yourself to a particular goal, task, or relationship, and executing decisions with purpose. Without commitment, it is easy to decide and then become distracted, lose motivation, or give up when faced with threats or difficulties. If you are only halfhearted about your commitment, your follow-through is usually less intense and may not be as effective as it could be. With commitment, you follow through on your decisions in spite of the challenges or obstacles that may arise. Commitment provides the necessary focus and drive to overcome obstacles and achieve your goals and brings a sense of purpose and fulfillment to your life.

When you shift from considering a decision to a state of commitment, you can proceed without reservation or too much concern with potential consequences. When Frankl was at Auschwitz, he and other prisoners were ordered to go to a cleansing station and toss their valuables onto blankets on the ground. Frankl rebelled and hid his two most valuable items in his jacket. Unfortunately, he was ordered to throw his clothes into a pile and his most treasured possessions were lost. Frankl found meaning through committing to his decision even though the consequences were not what he had hoped.

David Lopez, who will be introduced in Chapter 7, found meaning in committing to his decisions. He describes one example as follows:

> I never had a purpose, and there was no direction in my life at all. I lived only in the moment and was sent to prison as a result. Then I began to see my son on the same path as I had taken, and I decided to help him change the direction of his life. The effort has been difficult. We had a rough start when I got out of prison and there were years when we didn't talk, but we are working on it and our relationship is improving. I've made some decisions that have helped, and he's currently living in a mobile home I purchased. We talk almost every day, and our relationship gives meaning and purpose to my life. And I'm committed to seeing this continue.

It's been said that "doing things halfway is the mother of everything that can go wrong." When you want to succeed, you invest fully in your decisions and your purpose. One can't afford to only be "involved." Being involved means you are not committed, and if you're not committed, your purpose won't see the light of day.

Maintain a Spiritual Connection

Spirituality is the belief in something beyond the self; a higher power or a connection to others and the universe. It is the human spirit being grasped, sustained, and connected to something larger than self. Exploring spirituality can help you find purpose and meaning in life and consider philosophical questions such as "What is the meaning of life?" and "What purpose does my life serve?"

A spiritual connection reaches deep within you, allowing you to tap into your inner self, connect with others and with something greater than yourself, and embrace the vastness of the universe. It helps you navigate through the ups and downs, and experience a sense of joy, contentment, and fulfillment, while providing a sense of purpose and meaning in your life.

Frankl believed his connection to a spiritual dimension provided him with a sense of purpose and ultimately kept him alive. On one occasion while at Auschwitz, he was ordered to pick up clothes from a pile on the floor that had belonged to prisoners who were murdered in the gas chambers. He picked up a thin, torn coat with a scrap of paper in the pocket that was a torn page from the Jewish prayer book. On it was written the prayer Frankl had heard his father say every day as a young boy, which included "Hear, O Israel: The LORD our God, the LORD is one. Love the LORD your God with all your heart and with all your soul and with all your strength" (Deuteronomy 6:4–5). Frankl later wrote that this prayer (the "Shema," the centerpiece of the daily morning and evening prayer services, considered by some the most essential prayer in all of Judaism, and his connection to a spiritual realm) challenged him to live according to what he had written and to practice what he preached. On another occasion, while Frankl was shoveling snow, he was struggling to find meaning for the great suffering in his life. He heard a victorious "Yes" and at that exact moment looked up and a light from a farmhouse in the distance went on. The light turning on coincided with his inner voice telling him that life does have a purpose, which strengthened Frankl's desire to continue living.

Frankel's experiences with spiritual connections, like the note in the pocket and the farmhouse light, seem to have resulted from events that could be attributed to synchronicity. This may be true for you as well. Just taking the time to quiet your mind and focus inward will allow you to tap into a deeper sense of self-awareness, connect with the spiritual essence within you, feel a connection with the universe, and gain a deeper understanding of your place in it. Reading materials on spiritual awakening and engaging in meditation and mindfulness techniques can help in deepening your spiritual connection. Incorporating such practices into daily life helps your spiritual connection become stronger and more meaningful and fosters a life filled with purpose, fulfillment, and a deep sense of shalom.

CREATE AND CHASE GOALS

You may want to or need to change your life. Perhaps you have either behaved badly, or had your life disrupted by the bad behavior of others or by circumstances outside your control. Such difficult situations most likely started small, grew over time, and became complex, messy affairs that were difficult to resolve. Changing from such a life to a life of shalom is difficult and uncertain. It's a journey, not an event. It's like driving a car on an unfamiliar road. It's not easy or straightforward, but instead is filled with bumps, detours, curves, crossroads, and a myriad of other problems that often make it almost impossible to know what to do and when to do it. Changing your life has so many turns and crossroads that it's hard to find your destination. You need a map, or a GPS navigation system, to guide you.

Personal goals are a guide for your journey. They help you determine what you really want, where you'd like to go, and who you would like to become. They give you a sense of direction that helps you decide what you need to do and provides a path for getting there. Goals also help you stay motivated—focused, determined, and committed—and make it easier to measure your progress and see how far you've come.

Frankl wrote in *Man's Search for Meaning*, "Any attempt to restore a man's inner strength in the camp had first to succeed in showing him some future goal. . . .Whenever there was an opportunity for it, one had to give them a *why*—an aim—for their lives, in order to strengthen them to bear the terrible *how* of their existence. Woe to him who saw no more sense in his life, no aim, no purpose, and therefore no point in carrying on. He was soon lost."[12]

Any individual aiming to change from a difficult, troubled, or meaningless life to a life of purpose needs to lay out a path by establishing some supporting goals. You will need to start from where you are, but after that nothing is predictable. Both your goals and your process should be your own, and you need to be clear about where you're going (your purpose), explore, think, test, adopt, reject, and most importantly, expect to go through various parts of the process again and again. Your purpose in life probably developed over a long time, and it probably will take a long time to accomplish it.

Goals can be unwritten and informal, a mental understanding and commitment to do certain things that are necessary to accomplish life's purpose. However, it's often said that an unwritten goal is merely a wish, and scientific and anecdotal evidence shows that written goals are much more likely to lead to success. Writing goals activates your subconscious to look for opportunities. It helps create a vision in your mind of how you want to be in the future, helps you see the objective of the goal and understand the difference it will make in your life, and drives change in your actions to accomplish it. When you write down your goals you set an intention and declare "this is what I want to achieve." Chapter 11 briefly outlines the SMART process for goal setting and discusses goals in more detail.

As you take practical action toward your goals, opportunities arise, people appear, and the universe begins to align to bring you what you want—just when you need it—as though driven by synchronistic forces. Your purpose then becomes more than a wish. It becomes a series of actions that are important when standing alone, but when combined foster accomplishing your purpose. The first of these we will discuss is living by moral codes, addressed in Chapter 7.

QUESTIONS FOR REFLECTION

1. What is your purpose in life?
2. How does serving others serve you?
3. How do you commit to a purpose?
4. What does spiritual communication mean to you?
5. What is the difference between your purpose and a goal?

7
LIVING BY MORAL CODES

Now for this very reason also, applying all diligence, in your faith supply moral excellence, and in your moral excellence, knowledge. (2 Peter 1:5)

Each of us no doubt has done something in our lifetime we are not proud of. We had a sense of ambiguity, or worse, as to whether it was right or wrong and we now wish we hadn't done it. Or perhaps we are involved in something now that we are pretty sure isn't good, but we haven't yet reached the point where we are willing to give it up. Sometimes we need help in determining what is good and bad or right and wrong, and sometimes we're pretty sure we know the answer but we need help in disciplining ourself to do the right thing. We need to be governed by moral codes that set a standard for day to day living and for finding the peace, purity, wholeness, welfare, and prosperity characterized by a life of shalom. This chapter focuses on moral codes of the Old Testament, Jesus Christ, and the New Testament apostles as guidelines for doing what is right and good, transforming one's life, and finding a life of shalom.

Using biblical teachings to help you find a life of shalom that includes wholeness, welfare, contentment, and prosperity may sound a little like advocating the "prosperity gospel" and the claim of certain TV preachers and suburban megachurches that faith contains an implicit promise of earthly reward, and that God will give believers their heart's desires: money in the bank, a healthy body, a thriving family, and boundless happiness. While I have serious doubts about the validity of this proposition,

I do not here take a position on the matter. Instead, this chapter presents the Ten Commandments, the Sermon on the Mount, and the command to love as moral codes that guide your choices and behavior and suggest ways for you to do your part in worshipping God and dealing with others. The Biblical codes teach which acts, attitudes, and personal character traits are appropriate or inappropriate, good or bad, helpful or hurtful; and how to live, move from how things are to how they ought to be, and live a moral life that is Christ-like, pleasing to God, and characterized by shalom.

Morality in a contemporary society is both an objective and subjective concept. Many moral codes, norms, and precepts are objective truths, called moral absolutes. But individuals must make choices in life, which often involve the subjective dimension of morality. People often disagree about what is right and wrong, but most would probably agree that morality is the glue that binds societies and communities together. Without morality, people would live in a chaotic, selfish, and violent world where no one would care about the consequences of their actions or the well-being of others. At its core, morality is concerned with rights, responsibilities, what it means to live an ethical life, and how people make moral decisions. It promotes social harmony, cooperation, and justice, as well as respect for human dignity and rights. Moral codes encourage people to consider how their actions might affect others and to treat people the way they themselves want to be treated. When you share moral values, it's easier to work together toward common goals, and achieve more together than any one person could alone. While not always perfectly applied, morals can lead to the expansion of rights, the fair treatment of more groups over time, and the type of behavior that makes community life possible.

Laws often follow moral values. As society's views on right and wrong evolve, so do the laws established to govern behavior. When moral codes are widely accepted, they shape cultural norms and laws to support stability, safety, and well-being for all people. Things generally agreed to be unethical, like murder, theft, and fraud, are punished. Laws protect rights and values we hold dear, like freedom of speech, equal treatment, and property ownership. Our sense of justice is closely tied to morality, as moral reasoning determines what kind of consequence is fair and appropriate. Punishment should fit the crime, based on the gravity of the immoral act. More serious moral transgressions, like violent crimes, warrant harsher punishment. Lesser acts, like traffic violations, receive smaller penalties.

Reciprocity and empathy are key drivers of moral behavior. Reciprocity exists when you treat others a certain way and in turn they treat you the same way. You have empathy when you imagine yourself in the position of others and can feel their suffering, hopes, and desires. These influences lead you to believe that what applies to you should apply to others as well, which fosters moral treatment of others.

A "nature versus nurture" debate exists as to what drives people's morals. Numerous studies show that that they stem from basic human emotions and people are born with an innate sense of morality. Studies also show that nurturing, largely in the form of positive parenting that reinforces and rewards good behavior, correlates with a stronger sense of responsibility and morality in the children. Thus, parents can foster morality in children. But sometimes they don't.

David Lopez is a case in point. One of his earliest memories of his mother was her lying on the bathroom floor, going into convulsions, foaming at the mouth, with a needle sticking out of her arm. A key memory of his dad was of him beating his mother. She died when David was eleven and after that he bounced around from home to home, from relationship to relationship—hooked on smoking, drinking beer and other alcohol, and doing drugs. He says, "My lifestyle was not really suffering because everyone around me did it."

Then things got worse. David was convicted of burglary, assault, possession, and possession with intent to distribute and was incarcerated for ten years. After his release, he committed and was convicted of similar offenses and incarcerated again for two additional years.

David celebrated his tenth anniversary of sobriety during the time we were working together on the writing of this chapter. He reflected on his life as follows:

Today is ten years sober for me.

Back in 2014, I was arrested for the last time and began my transformation. I remember April 15, 2014, well.

I had been up on drugs and high as a kite for three days straight.

I had been on the run from the cops for over seven months.

I had jumped bail and had bounty hunters chasing me down. I knew one day I would get caught, I mean, I literally wasn't trying to hide after jumping bond. By this point I had lost everything and was surviving on the hustle to keep me going.

The cops jumped out on me. I was surrounded by the gulf coast area violent fugitive offender task force.

I had dope in every pocket.

I was busted. Sitting in the back of the cop car hit different this time. Cops had jumped out as soon as I got out of the car to go make a drop. Someone somewhere had snitched me out and they knew where I would be. My girlfriend at the time was still in the car and she was surrounded by about five officers with guns drawn screaming at her to get out of the car. She was frozen. After a few minutes she stepped out and everything ended.

That was the best night's sleep I had ever had!

When I woke up and went to court I had four felony charges pending.

No bond.

At that moment I knew my life would never be the same.

David participated in Bridges To Life at the Holliday Unit, where he met Richard Lopez, then the prison Chaplain and later the Head Chaplain of the Texas prison system and a BTL Regional Coordinator. Richard became aware of the close relationship David had had with his mother and once asked him, "When are you going to let your mother rest in peace?" Thinking of his mother and of Richard's question motivated him to hold on during his incarceration.

David continued his story:

When I got out, I literally had only the clothes on my back. I was fortunate to have been able to parole out to a good home, for a couple of months at least. The day I was asked to leave that home I was told they had done enough to help me get my feet under me, which was true. I ended up on my father's living room floor because the couch was very uncomfortable. I was literally at bottom, but I knew that from that day I would not drink, or smoke, or put in anything that would get me sent back to prison.

David went to work for his uncle. He described it:

I worked in stucco, mixing mortar all day directly under the sun. When it would rain we couldn't work, when it was too cold we couldn't work. It was on those days that I would look for work and found a job, and lifelong friend, that would begin the transformation to the man I am striving to be. Things have not always been easy, there have been many struggles along the way. But life has changed for the better. Practicing BTL principles has allowed me to be blessed beyond measure.

Shortly before David's release, a prison chaplain had mentioned that when he was released, David should contact the Work-Faith Connection, a Christ-centered not-for-profit organization that helps men and women find jobs and begin productive lives through work. David contacted the organization and they found him a job. He didn't have a car when he started, but was finally able to purchase a truck from a co-worker for three payments of $500 each. Once David had a truck, he needed a driver's license. When he went to the driver's license office, he noticed that the Work-Faith Connection office was across the street. He walked over and arranged to take one of their classes and use their other services as needed. This led to a better job as a forklift operator at a corrugated box company at $11.00 per hour, which was higher pay than pitching cement. He worked in that job for a couple of years, then became safety and quality manager, and then plant superintendent a year later. In 2022 he switched jobs, and currently is operations manager for a Georgia-based company that operates paper mills and a recycling company, and is one of the top five corrugated box manufacturers, and the top privately held box company, in the country, He says:

> I continue to grow at work. Now I am operations manager with an immediate goal of becoming general manager. The organization I work for knew about my past. I spoke of it in my interview and they still allow me to grow. I can set the bar for future second chance employees.

David's personal life has improved as well. He says:

> I never had a purpose in life. There was no direction in it at all. I now have a son aged twenty and a child and stepchild who are younger. My main purpose is to be an example for my children, do the best I can for my family, and avoid a generational curse. The most difficult thing has been the relationship with my son, who saw the worst in me. I could see him on the same path as I had taken, and I wanted to change it, which meant I had to change myself and be a better father for my kids. My relationship with him has been difficult. We had a rough start when I got out of prison. There were years when we didn't talk, but we worked on it and it improved. I've been able to help him financially and he's currently living in the mobile home I purchased for him. We talk almost every day.

David summarizes his life today, several years after his release from incarceration:

> I try to do the best I can and be there for my kids. I want them to know that they can call on me at any time. I can relax and live a normal productive life. No one is looking over my shoulder. I have a cup of coffee. No one in the household has to worry. I can provide. No one is smoking up the rent money. I'm trying to do the right things. I love being there for them—mentally, physically, and spiritually. I dreamed of being where I am today. I've never said this to anyone before, and it really feels good.

David, by and large, is living a life of shalom like so many people aspire to. Believing in God and aiming to do His will provides a practical moral compass for finding such a life. The Bible describes the type of life one needs to avoid mistakes, pain, and suffering like David experienced. It establishes standards of right and wrong, good and bad, and provides a goal to shoot for and guidance in choices for change from a life that is off track to one of shalom. The Ten Commandments, the Sermon on the Mount, which includes the Beatitudes, the Lord's Prayer, and the Golden Rule, and the great commandment to love God and one's neighbor provided this important guidance for David's life—and will for your life as well. Each of them is discussed below.

THE TEN COMMANDMENTS

Recorded in Exodus 20 and Deuteronomy 5, the Ten Commandments offer one of the Bible's great moral codes, or blueprints for living. God revealed the Ten Commandments to Moses as a list of religious precepts engraved on two tablets of stone. These statutes were collectively meant to show the Israelites God's standard of holiness and give them a glimpse of God's character.

The first four commandments deal with the Israelites', and our, responsibility to God. They command that we have no other gods, make no idols, not take the name of the Lord in vain, and keep the Sabbath day holy.

The final six commandments address the Israelites' responsibility toward each other and provide a moral code for people today.

- Honor your mother and father.
- Don't murder.
- Don't commit adultery.
- Don't steal.
- Don't give false testimony.
- Don't covet.

The Ten Commandments provide guiding principles that apply universally across changing circumstances and guide people in living a moral and ethical life. They are part of God's moral law and are a key tool in helping you distinguish right from wrong, honor moral absolutes, and identify truths. The Ten Commandments show you what God wants; they show you what God is like, tell you what matters to Him, and set the stage for true freedom and a life of shalom. These laws serve as guardians, guardrails, and teaching tools to help you understand God's expectations—and generally what is acceptable in our society. They can be used as a tool for self-reflection and understanding how your actions relate to honoring God and loving your neighbor.

These Commandments are central to the ethics of the New Testament. In Mark 10:17, for example, a man comes to Jesus and asks, "What must I do to inherit eternal life?" Jesus says to him, "You know the commandments. You shall not murder, you shall not commit adultery, you shall not steal, you shall not give false testimony, you shall not defraud, honor your father and mother."

David played pretty loose with the Ten Commandments in his early life, as confirmed by his incarceration based on his conviction of burglary, assault, possession, and possession with intent to distribute. He says,

> The Ten Commandments? That's a tough one. In my addiction, I didn't honor my mother and father, I served my addiction until the money ran out, then begged everyone for forgiveness. I wanted what others had and did what I had to do to get it. There was no honor in that. Now that I've gotten clean, I'm still struggling to keep the Commandments. I have the same drive as I did in my addiction. I'm going to hustle at work and do my best to build for my family and myself. The only difference is I do so in an honorable way. To be clear, life hasn't gotten any easier. But with God in my heart, I know things will never be the same as they were.

In summary, the Ten Commandments are like traffic laws. These laws may seem limiting at times, but they provide a way of law, order, and safety. People stop and go. People slow down when driving by schools and stop for school buses. When they drive on a switchback on a mountain pass, guardrails prevent them from plunging to an untimely death. They help people travel freely and safely. Similarly, the Ten Commandments will point you in the right direction and help keep you on track. You cannot keep the commandments fully or perfectly, but they show you the way to live, the way to love your neighbor, and the way to love God with all your heart and soul. And this will rebound, as it has for David, to a better life for you.

THE SERMON ON THE MOUNT

The Sermon on the Mount, found in Matthew, Chapters 5–7, is a collection of sayings spoken by Jesus to his core disciples and a crowd of others that emphasizes his moral teachings. In many ways, Jesus' teachings in the Sermon on the Mount represent the major ideals of the Christian life. For example, He taught about subjects such as prayer, justice, care for the needy, handling the religious law, divorce, fasting, judging other people, salvation, and much more. Jesus demanded righteousness in our hearts as well as in our deeds, and a life of discipline based on a new law of love, even to enemies, as opposed to the old law of retribution. The Sermon on the Mount includes the Beatitudes (Matthew 5:3–12), the Lord's Prayer (Matthew 6:9–13), and the Golden Rule (Matthew 7:12).

The Beatitudes

The Sermon on the Mount begins with the Beatitudes: sayings of Jesus that present a set of ideals that focus on love and humility rather than demands and force. They echo the highest ideals of Jesus' teachings on spirituality and compassion. Matthew 5:3–10 reads:

> [3]Blessed are the poor in spirit,
>   for theirs is the Kingdom of Heaven.
> [4]Blessed are those who mourn,
>   for they will be comforted.
> [5]Blessed are the meek,
>   for they will inherit the Earth.
> [6]Blessed are those who hunger and thirst for righteousness,
>   for they will be satisfied.

[7]Blessed are the merciful,
   for they will be shown mercy.
[8]Blessed are the pure in heart,
   for they will see God.
[9]Blessed are the peacemakers,
   for they will be called the Sons of God.
[10]Blessed are those who are persecuted because of righteousness,
   for theirs is the Kingdom of Heaven.

Beginning with the phrase, "Blessed are . . ." each saying speaks of a blessing or "divine favor" that will be bestowed on the person who possesses a certain character quality. The phrase "blessed are" in each Beatitude implies a current state of happiness or well-being—as in a state of shalom. The Beatitudes introduce and set the tone for Jesus' Sermon on the Mount by emphasizing the humble state of humans and the righteousness of God.

The Lord's Prayer

The Lord's Prayer is a Christian prayer that Jesus taught as the way to pray and request God's guidance and protection. It summarizes what Christians believe and how they should live. The traditional form of the prayer can be found in Matthew 6:9–15. The first three of the seven petitions in Matthew address God; the other four are related to human needs and concerns in our daily life.

[9]"This, then, is how you should pray:
   "'Our Father in heaven,
   hallowed be your name,
[10]your kingdom come,
   your will be done,
   on earth as it is in heaven.
[11]Give us today our daily bread.
[12]And forgive us our debts,
   as we also have forgiven our debtors.

¹³And lead us not into temptation,
> but deliver us from the evil one.

¹⁴For if you forgive other people when they sin against you, your heavenly Father will also forgive you. **15** But if you do not forgive others their sins, your Father will not forgive your sins.

The prayer recognizes divine things first, and yet clearly asserts the ethical and social relations of life. When we pray, we trust God to provide our daily bread—to meet our needs. We depend on God to provide what we need for today. Tomorrow we can renew our dependence by coming to him in prayer once again. We ask God to forgive our sins when we pray. We search our hearts and recognize that we need his forgiveness. We need strength from God to resist temptation and stay in tune with His guidance to avoid anything that will tempt us to sin.

The "Golden Rule"

The "Golden Rule" requires a good and positive life that honors others and avoids the hurt many of us so often feel or impose on others. It teaches, "So in everything, do to others what you would have them do to you, for this sums up the Law and the Prophets." (Matthew 7:12) This "rule" lays out the ethical principle of treating other people as one prefers to be treated: an ethical stance that seems to include "love thy neighbor," "turn the other cheek," and other similar ideas that revolve around themes such as empathy, selflessness, reciprocity, and love that are at the foundations of most ethical systems. The Golden Rule encompasses the empathic essence of morality and teaches that you should recognize the dignity of your fellow man and not forget you are capable of inflicting immoral actions. It instructs you to put yourself in your neighbor's place, and guides your behavior accordingly; assuming that you are wise enough not to make any foolish wishes and good enough not to make any evil ones.

Jesus made it clear that His followers should live in a noticeably different way than other people, and they should hold to a much higher standard of conduct than is expected in society—the standard of love and selflessness that Jesus Himself embodied. Thus, for example, we are taught not only to avoid murder, but also to avoid anger; not to commit adultery, but also not to look lustfully on another; to turn the other cheek when someone hits us, and other great teachings that help us address our inner beings as well as our behavior.

David Lopez's take on the Sermon on the Mount is that that "though I've been through plenty of trials as a result of my actions, I can rejoice because better days are coming. No matter what I've been through, God has a purpose for my life. I want to inherit the kingdom of God and must do my part."

LOVE

We have discussed a number of important commandments in Scripture that comprise a moral code for our lives, and there are other codes in our culture that people should follow. According to scripture, a lawyer and expert in the law asked Jesus what the most important commandment is. Jesus responded, " 'Love the Lord your God with all your heart and with all your soul and with all your mind.' This is the first and greatest commandment. And the second is like it: 'Love your neighbor as yourself.' All the Law and the Prophets hang on these two commandments." (Matthew 22: 37–40)

Chapter 3 discussed agape love as the highest, most pure form of love: selfless sacrificial service to others that accepts and embraces the wholeness of each person without reservation. Jesus quotes from Leviticus 19 and explains that loving your neighbor also includes sharing with the poor and the alien; compassion, honesty, and justice in your relationships with others; impartiality; refusal to gossip or slander; an absence of malice toward anyone and a refusal to bear a grudge; never putting another's life at risk; never taking private vengeance upon another; and not stealing, nor dealing falsely, nor lying to another.

When Jesus identified the two most important commandments— love of God and love of neighbor, He gave you a blueprint on how you should live and simplified following God and obeying his commands in everyday life. He implies that you need to first love God if you are to love other people. If you love God with all your heart, soul, and mind, you are transformed and begin to love others as yourself. It goes without saying that you need to show more love for others, less hate, more grace for others, and less judgment. If you love God fully, with all your heart, soul, and mind, as Jesus teaches, you will find that you are able to see others through the eyes of Jesus. You can lay down your grievances and let God deal with your enemies.

Your morality—your sense of right and wrong—has a direct effect on how you view yourself and interact with others, and it shapes your thoughts and experiences each day. When you act in accordance with moral values, you feel good about yourself. You have a sense of integrity and self-worth. Guilt, shame, and regret are minimized. In the end, living morally leads to living well. Acting with integrity, kindness, and goodwill paves the way for better health, happiness, well-being—and for forgiving others.

Questions For Reflection

1. Which moral code most affects your life?
2. Discuss the roles of reciprocity and empathy in morality?
3. Which of the beatitudes is the most relevant to you?
4. How does love combine the other moral laws?
5. Why should you follow the moral laws of the Bible?

8

FORGIVING AND RECONCILING

Then Peter came up and said to him, "Lord, how often will my brother sin against me, and I forgive him? As many as seven times?" Jesus said to him, "I do not say to you seven times, but seventy-seven times." (Matthew 18:21–22)

Judy Dunn learned about forgiveness and reconciliation in perhaps the hardest of all ways. She grew up in Arkansas, had a daughter at age seventeen, graduated high school a year early, and moved with her military husband to Oklahoma and then to New Mexico. After a couple of intervening stops, by late 1989 Judy was a single mother of three girls, living in Round Rock, Texas, and working for the IBM company. Her oldest daughter had grown up and moved away from home, and the youngest lived with her father. Kelly, the middle daughter, lived with Judy in their small suburban house in a nice middle-class neighborhood. Thirteen years old and in the seventh-grade Talented and Gifted Program, Kelly was almost five feet tall, with a slender, athletic build, light brown hair hanging a little below her shoulders, beautiful sky-blue eyes, and a perpetual smile on her face. She and her mom had a very special relationship.

The evening of December 2, 1989, Kelly, predictably dressed in grey athletic sweats from school, was in their driveway playing basketball with Terrence, her twelve-year-old friend and neighbor. Around 6:00 p.m., Judy went to the front door and called her name. There was no answer. Judy began a search. Shortly thereafter, her friend, David, arrived to pick her up for an evening out. She invited him in but told him they could not leave until she found Kelly. A couple of hours later, Judy called the police and gave them a missing person report. She spent the remainder of the night pacing the floors. At daylight on Sunday morning, David started walking the neighborhood again, and Judy began calling everyone again.

Around 9:00 a.m., Terrence's dad knocked on Judy's door. Just standing there on the porch, gripping his gut, he exclaimed, "Judy. Judy, I found her. I found her."

Judy ran into the front yard, thinking there was good news.

Terrence's dad continued, "I went out to get some firewood and I saw Kelly." Then he led Judy to a woodpile in his backyard.

Judy looked at the stack of firewood and saw Kelly laying in the grass, a bloody mass on the top of her head, her sweat tops pulled up, her back badly scraped. Judy says, "I looked and just started screaming at the top of my lungs."

Judy called the police. When the police arrived, they investigated the situation and as delicately as possible told Judy, "Your daughter's dead. She's been murdered, and we think we know who did it. It's the boy next door."

Judy responded, "No. You made a horrible mistake. Terrence is Kelly's friend."

Terrence later said that during their game Kelly left to answer her phone. He went to his house and called her number, assuming she had dumped him for a better option. He asked her to come to his house, and when she did, Terrence stabbed her ninety-seven times with a serrated kitchen knife.

Terrence claimed he had bumped his nose, and all the blood was from a nosebleed. No one believed him. He was arrested and taken to a juvenile detention facility, where he admitted to his dad what he had done, so oblivious to the gravity of the situation that he thought he would be home for Christmas.

Amazingly, although Terrence was in the juvenile facility longer than he hoped to be, he remembers these as some of the happiest times he had ever experienced. He says that as a twelve-year-old, he didn't understand the enormity of his action, the harm he had caused, or the likely consequences. His parents came to see him almost every day, and he received the first hugs he could remember. He reveled in the attention and affection he received.

Terrence was initially charged in family court with criminal mischief. The charge was later changed to murder, and trial was set for Kerrville, Texas—a change of venue because of all the publicity surrounding the murder. Judy attended every day of the two-week trial and explains, "I became very angry: at Terrence for what he had done, at the defense attorney for the way he mistreated Kelly's friends who testified, and at the world generally. I was particularly disgusted with Terrence, who seemed to just sit next to his attorney and stare at the ceiling with no remorse at all for what he did to Kelly and the devastation it caused to my family and friends."

Terrence attended each day of the trial but did not testify. His parents were not present, as they left town for several months to avoid testifying against their son. Several of Judy's relatives and friends attended in a show of support.

Terrence was convicted, given a thirty-year sentence, and sent to the Texas Youth Commission facility at Giddings, Texas, where he would remain until he reached age eighteen. Judy considered the thirty-year sentence a slap in the face. Her mission became to keep Terrence incarcerated for as many of the thirty years of his sentence as she could. She appealed to the Texas legislature and a law was enacted to extend the maximum term of such sentences by ten years, although the extension was not retroactive and did not apply to Terrence. She protested at each of his parole hearings until 2018. Judy says, "My argument was, it doesn't matter if he was 12, 22, 42, or 82. My child is still just as dead."

At Giddings State School, Terrence was incarcerated with the worst youth offenders in the state. For the first time, he had to deal with the reality of what he had done to his good friend. He says, "Having to deal with the facts of my crime every day and being made to look into the mirror to see who I really was nearly broke me when I was fourteen years old. It finally set in my mind what I had done."

Terrence experienced about six months of severe depression and even asked some friends to help him kill himself. Then he met a Social Service Administrator who, according to Terrence, "saw me as a broken little boy who needed help and counseled me and my mother and father. She helped me understand who I was and how I became the violent person I had become."

Judy couldn't begin to wrap her head around how Kelly's friend could kill her. She says:

> I was in shock, and it lasted a really long time. For the first four months, I just tried to figure out what to do with myself, as I went from being a parent of an incredibly active daughter to being alone. I focused on all the wonderful things about Kelly—her inclusive and outgoing personality, academic accomplishments, successes in volleyball, basketball, karate, and as a competitive gymnast, and her participation in dance, choir, and other extracurricular activities. I was able to thank God that He had allowed me to have thirteen years, and a very close and wonderful relationship, with my extraordinary daughter. I remember some "out of body experiences" where it seemed I was just watching myself go through the motions of living, but I was so numb I wasn't sure what I was doing. I did things that most people wouldn't do. I didn't cry—never have—because I was scared if I ever started, I wouldn't be able to stop. I attended functions Kelly would have been involved in with her friends. On her birthday, I took a boy whose birthday was the day after hers to get pizza and to a music store. I couldn't do it for my own child, and he was the closest I could get. I went back to work the week following Kelly's funeral, because I didn't want to stay home and grieve alone, and the only place I felt normal and safe was when I was at work. When I was outside of my work life, I didn't know what to do with myself.

For the first few years after the murder, Judy lived in fear of Terrence being released and showing up at her door with a gun to finish the job. He was considered for parole every three years, and prior to each hearing Judy spent several months gathering information to contest his release. She was so angry and hurt that she thought only bad things about Terrence, and she thought about them continually. She says, "I knew it was wrong and that as a Christian I couldn't act on such thoughts. This continued over the years with a lot of bitterness and hurt. I knew I had to forgive, but I couldn't. I just kept praying about it."

One of the things Judy did to help deal with the trauma of her situation was to volunteer with the newly formed Bridges To Life organization. She told her story and served as a small group facilitator at the Kyle Correctional Facility, the women's Ellen Halbert unit, and the Travis County State Jail.

When he was eighteen, Terrence was shipped to the Wallace prison unit. It was a very violent and scary atmosphere, comprised, according to Terrence, of "murderers, rapists, thieves, gang bangers, dope dealers, and heartless men who knew nothing but a life of survival among the worst criminals in the state of Texas." Terrence affiliated with prison "cliques" and at one time was the number four person in a gang's chain of command.

After roughly four years, Terrence was transferred to the Wynne unit, which he found to be quite peaceful and settled as compared to Wallace; and then six years later to the Coffield unit, where he says the atmosphere was even more toxic than at Wallace. He describes these times as follows: "I was engaged in prison contraband, smoking weed, doing drugs and I was just doing a lot of things that would invite trouble into my life. Most of the stuff that I was doing was because I was ashamed of who I was, and I was trying to change and reinvent myself—not be the coward I felt in my heart. I lived certain lifestyles that I thought would help shield me from some of the things other people experienced."

While at the Coffield unit Terrence was stabbed in an altercation with another inmate and received a serious gash on his arm that required twenty stitches, plus busted lips, two chipped teeth, and two loose teeth. He was sent to isolation pending an investigation of what had happened, where an incident occurred that he says changed his life forever. He briefly described this incident in *Chasing Redemption*, a short book he wrote while he was incarcerated.

> On December 17th, 2006, I sat on my bunk in isolation with my back against the wall as I looked down on my bandaged left forearm, when a sudden realization out of nowhere washed over me.
>
> I thought about Kelly and the tragedy that took place exactly seventeen years prior. I tortured myself by reviewing every action like a movie running in my head and I cried as I had never cried before. My cries were for Kelly and the terrible pain and suffering I had inflicted upon her. Tears flowed for Kelly's family and friends, people whose lives would never be the same, because I altered those lives in such a tragic way. I cried for Kelly's mother. And yes, I cried for my own regret and shame, and I even cried for the little boy I once was. I fell to my knees and began to pray.
>
> I prayed and asked God for forgiveness like I had done so many times before. I prayed for the opportunity to tell Kelly's mother that I was sorry for all the wrong I had committed against her. I asked God for the opportunity to show her the sincerity of my remorse, because out of everyone I did not want Kelly's mother to hate me.
>
> I had not shed a tear in prison for a long time, for I was afraid to cry and show weakness. But as I lay down to sleep after my awakening, I felt a sense of peace. My burden did not feel as heavy as before and I could only think that this time God was listening to me and I knew in my heart that Kelly had heard me too and I really believed each was forgiving me.

Judy continued to worry about what might happen after Terrence was released. In anticipation of his possible parole, she and David, then her husband, moved to Washington just to be safe. Judy started the BTL program in the state and initiated programs in six prisons. She found that working with these projects gave her the same type of peace that she had experienced when volunteering in Texas.

FORGIVENSS

Forgiveness is granting free pardon or giving up resentment for a hurt or debt against a person. Forgiveness is a gift we give ourselves. It removes the hurt or injustice from our heart so that the negative emotions of the wound no longer dwell in us. It overcomes the hurt with mercy and love. We seek forgiveness when we have a sorrow in our soul for what we have done or failed to do, with a desire to not act in a similar way in the future. We forgive others when we remove from our hearts the impact the other person's words or deeds had on our lives. It does not mean one forgets the hurt, but they leave the offense behind and move on to a better future, difficult as it often is. In the fall of 2016, the first crack appeared in Judy's armor of resistance to forgiving Terrence. She was facilitating BTL projects at Washington State Reformatory each Tuesday afternoon and at the Twin Rivers Prison each Tuesday night. Both groups were on week ten, Forgiveness, and were discussing Patricia Stonestreet, the brutal murder of her wonderful daughter Lisa, and how Patricia and her family had forgiven Lisa's murderer. Near the end of the afternoon session at the Reformatory, seemingly out of the blue, an inmate leaned forward, looked Judy directly in the eyes, and said, with confidence and respect, "Judy. . . .This forgiveness stuff. When are you going to forgive Terrence?"

Judy says:

That hit me where it hurt. It was like a spear into my heart. I knew I needed to forgive just like I was asking the BTL participants to. I'd been praying about it for years, but I just was not there. All ten guys in the group were staring at me as I explained that I often had trouble accepting that forgiveness does not mean forgetting, and I was not able to forget what had happened to Kelly. I looked into their eyes one by one, called each by his first name, and said, "I apologize to you. I am a hypocrite. I come in here and I talk to you about forgiveness, and I haven't done it myself. I am so sorry. I have thought about it, and I have prayed about it, but I just have not been able to let go."

That evening at the Twin River prison, a man in her small group flab-bergasted her with, "Forgiveness, huh? So when are you going to forgive Terrence?"

Judy explains:

I was overwhelmed. I knew that communication between inmates at the two facilities was strictly prohibited, so it was very unlikely to have been planned. I felt like God was saying, "OK, Judy, I'm right here with you. It's your time." I looked directly into the eyes of the ten men in this group and apologized to them as I had to the guys at the Reformatory. The men prayed for me. I said to myself that I was finished with this and totally turned it over to God. There was not a dry eye in the room.

I walked out of that prison that night feeling like I had a ten-ton weight lifted off my shoulders. I have not regretted it for a single minute. I tell people in my BTL projects not to be a Judy. Holding the hate and not forgiving was eating me alive, from inside out, affecting my relationships with people and God, and changing who I was as a person. That experience was a pivotal point in my life.

Judy had been praying that Terrence would participate in a BTL program. What she didn't know at the time, and later learned, was that during that same week he was participating in week ten, Forgiveness, in the Ramsey prison in Texas. Her prayer was answered. Terrence graduated from BTL later that year.

Terrence says that when BTL was offered on his unit, he prayed on it and signed up without really knowing what to expect. He didn't expect to be enlightened about the victims of crime that he had never given much thought to. He says:

Those of us who had committed violent crimes had never heard the other side of the story, the stories of the victims and the family and the community. When you are exposed to those stories it does some-thing to you. I began to empathize with victims of crime and learned that I had to accept responsibility for my crime. BTL motivated me to be open and honest about what I had done. It was a very powerful experience that helped me deal with the burden I had assumed. I still hate myself for what I did, but I'm not where I was before Bridges To Life.

The second milestone in Judy's forgiveness journey occurred about a year later when she decided she would not protest Terrence's parole review, feeling, *I'm done with that. I can't keep on doing this.*

Terrence was paroled in January 2019. In addition to Bridges To Life, he had completed the Christian-based Alpha and Voyager intervention programs, and an anger management program offered through his participation in a Gang Renunciation and Dissociation Program. He earned a GED certificate and a high school diploma, an associate degree in accounting, a bachelor's in psychology, and a master's in literature. He also met and fell in love with Camilla, a prison guard at the time, whom he married after his release.

Upon release, Terrence initially worked for his parent's trucking company and is now employed by Anthem Strong Families, a Dallas organization that aims "to see all families soar and succeed." He frequently speaks to groups of high school students about the consequences of violence.

Terrence says, "Life is hard for me and always is a struggle. Living every day of my life with what I did is hard for me. I have a wife, a two-year-old daughter, a four-year-old son, and a six-year-old stepdaughter. I try to be strong for them as I deal with things I've never been exposed to before."

Judy retired from IBM in 2016 and took a position on the staff of BTL as a Regional Coordinator. Three years later, she accepted a transfer and returned to Texas with a prime objective of establishing BTL programs in several prisons in the Lubbock area. She was still fearful of Terrence.

Even after the jumpstart by the BTL small groups in the Washington prisons, Judy continued to struggle with the complexities of forgiveness and whether, when, and how to forgive Terrence. She says, "I struggled with forgiveness for twenty-seven years. I knew as a Christian that God required it, but in the beginning the mother in me was afraid that if I forgave Terrence, I would start losing some of my wonderful memories of Kelly, and I was not willing to do it. In addition, I never saw a single bit of remorse from Terrence. I was not able to see my daughter grow up and be what she could be, and I couldn't have a relationship with her, so I stayed very bitter and angry toward Terrence. I thought he didn't care and wouldn't even acknowledge what he had done."

Forgiveness allows you to overcome intense negative reactions such as resentment, anger, hatred, and desire for revenge, which are caused when you have been wronged by another. Forgiveness is a choice: a decision and an internal change of heart, not an action or behavior—a difficult personal decision that you make in your own way and time. Sometimes you need to forgive someone and the next time they may need to forgive you. It is a lifelong process in the pursuit of a more Christ-like relationship among those who have hurt one another.

RECONCILIATION

Sometimes forgiveness focuses almost exclusively on an individual's ability to cope with their feelings or change their behavior. It is one-dimensional: I forgive you in my heart for what you did to me, and I feel better as a result and can move on with my life, but our relationship doesn't change. Forgiveness also can be a first step that leads to fuller, more mature forgiveness that involves many, often difficult, milestones, such as communication, confession, repentance, trust, and whatever other elements are necessary for two people to develop a communion between themselves and with God. This fuller forgiveness is multidimensional: I forgive you, you repent and change your life, we both are better, and we engage in an appropriate relationship. For many years, Judy was barely able to engage in even the one-dimensional form of forgiveness. Then the door opened to a form of communion between her and Terrence.

We can't force another to reconcile, but we can foster an environment for reconciliation and take a number of actions that make it more likely to happen. Often reconciliation is not possible because of the death of the person who harmed us, or it isn't safe to reconnect, and so forth, but forgiveness is always possible because we have the ability to forgive even if the person is never made aware of it.

The Victim Offender Mediation Dialogue (VOMD) process of the Texas Department of Criminal Justice (TDCJ) is a unique program that permits victims to request a structured, face-to-face meeting with "their" offender, if the offender agrees and admits guilt. Through VOMD, victims may say what needs to be said and receive answers to unanswered questions, which helps in their healing and recovery process. It also permits offenders, in the truest sense, to acknowledge that they are responsible and accountable for their crimes.

Judy requested a mediation dialog in 1996 and in 2016, but Terrence did not agree in either case. However, Judy again requested, and Terrence and the TDCJ agreed to a mediation session for August of 2020, which was quite unusual because it was after Terrence's release, and this is normally not done.

The mediation was the first time Judy had had any direct contact with Terrence since she observed him at his trial, and it was virtual, by Zoom. The conversation was calm and respectful, lasted almost four hours, and covered a wide range of topics with a heavy emphasis on issues raised by Judy. Each of them felt good about the discussion. The entire mediation, and one situation in particular, confirmed Judy's decision to forgive Terrence. She explains:

> During the mediation I saw him get sick to his stomach, throw up in a trash can, and cry like a baby because of what he was hearing. He acknowledged that he had made a horrible mistake and said he was so sorry for what he had done and would change it all if he could. If he had just given some indication of this early on it would have saved me so many years of fear and anger from all the horrible things I was imagining. That was life changing, and it changed everything for me. At that point I thought, OK *we're done. You and I don't need to be carrying this around anymore.* I told him that both of us needed to quit looking backwards and move forward with our lives.

The Bridges To Life organization holds fundraising events each year, and typically invites two or three former inmate participants to tell the attendees how BTL has affected them. Judy and Terrence were invited to speak at the events in Arlington and Houston a couple of years after the mediation. At Judy's request, the two of them were seated for dinner in Arlington at the same ten-person table—not together, but across from one another. Each was nervous, and Terrence was so tense that he couldn't eat his rubber chicken meal. They had a similar encounter a couple months later at the Houston luncheon, which was attended by Terrence's parents.

Terrence spoke first at each event. He described killing Kelly, talked a little about his life in prison and since his release, and told of how BTL had changed his life. Then he announced, "And now I have the honor of introducing Kelly's mother." The collective gasp of the audience was palpable, as though all the oxygen had been sucked from the room while people tried to decide if they had heard incorrectly, or just couldn't believe what they thought they had heard.

Terrence says, "We were standing there together in Arlington. I was nervous and wanted a protector, so I asked her if it was alright if I gave her a hug. She said yes. I felt very nervous, but we hugged." Judy and Terrence hugged again on the stage in Houston. This one seemed much more real and genuine.

Judy explained to the audience at each location:

When I forgave Terrence, I didn't forgive what he did—he stabbed Kelly ninety-seven times in the face and head with a serrated bread knife. But I forgave him as a person. I now can look at him as a troubled kid who took it out on the wrong person at the wrong time. Kelly just happened to be convenient. I don't think it was premeditated to the point that he planned it out for weeks or anything. I think it was one of those horrible, horrible, spur of the moment decisions. Looking back, if I had known that he was sorry for what he did, regretted it, and wished that he hadn't done it, I could have saved myself twenty-seven years of terrible feelings. My prayer all those years was just that he not hurt anyone else."

Following the Houston luncheon, Jim Buffington, BTL's Chief Operating Officer, arranged for Judy and Terrence to meet privately, with him and his wife Marilyn present. They spoke freely with one another. In the process, Judy told Terrence he needed to let go of all that had happened and move on with his life. Terrence asked what he could do to make up for what he had done, and Judy replied that the only thing she wanted him to do was to be a good father.

Jim sensed that both felt a sense of relief and release, and described the discussion as a very emotional, special time. Judy says she made progress in getting to know Terrence the man rather than Terrence the kid. Terrence says, "Facing Judy was the hardest thing I've ever done in my life, but also one of the greatest things that's ever happened to me."

Judy summarizes her forgiveness and reconciliation journey as follows: "I think that we as humans too easily hold on to grudges and hurts and to things that are hurting us. Forgiveness is not forgiving someone to let them off the hook so much as letting yourself off the hook. It's so easy to hold on to negative things and we're only hurting ourselves. If we can just give it to God and let him take over, then we're gonna be a lot happier and more satisfied."

Terrence says forgiveness from the people he has hurt the most is a gift from which he has benefited greatly, even though it was not necessarily for him. It relieved a burden he was carrying and became a steppingstone toward things that can be more positive.

We all want to be forgiven for our offenses and for hurting another if we are truly remorseful. Being forgiven and reconciling if feasible is part of the healing process. It shows there is sufficient goodness in us that someone else has judged us acceptable, allows us to begin to find peace, and fosters shalom in our life.

Terrence wrote in his prison book, "I hope to one day to be able to talk to the members of Kelly's family to answer their long-held questions and express my remorse," and later said, "I hope that one day I can receive a measure of forgiveness for my childhood actions because I truly do regret having hurt so many people. I now know the freedom and peace and great relief forgiveness brings, and I wish that for them, too."

Fortunately, for each of them, Judy granted Terrence that peace. His participation in the Victim Offender Mediation Dialogue, appearing with Judy at the BTL events, and meeting with her privately after the Houston luncheon suggests that he accepted her forgiveness. But he had another forgiveness issue to deal with: the question of forgiving himself for what he had done.

FORGIVING SELF

Does anyone have the right or authority to forgive himself or herself for hurting others? Reasonable people might disagree. Some say yes, we can and we should, while others say we cannot because it isn't our role and we have no authority to do it. It took Terrence a very long time to answer this question. It seemed to him that forgiving himself for his crime was the same as saying what he did was okay, and he knew it wasn't. Feeling guilty and ashamed felt better than feeling forgiven, so he was trapped in his own guilt and shame over what he did. He felt paralyzed and unable to get beyond his past.

Terrence accepted responsibility, acknowledged his accountability, repented, and confessed his crime to himself, God, Judy, and Kelly. He believed they had forgiven him, and he accepted their forgiveness. But he still struggled with forgiving himself. Forgiving himself was difficult and frustrating, because he lived with himself 24-7, and he didn't like the man staring back in the mirror. He knew he had done terrible things, and guilt and self-hatred prevented him from forgiving himself and becoming who he should be. However, he finally began to ask himself: *In light of all this forgiveness, who am I not to forgive me. Am I greater than God or Judy or Kelly? If they forgive me, who am I not to?*

Terrence came to accept that no one is perfect: we all make mistakes and bad decisions, and he needed to join the human race, where we all fail at some things and sometimes hurt other people. His was a terrible crime, but he wasn't the only one to have done such a thing, and he remembered that forgiving himself did not mean condoning what he had done. He had repented and accepted the forgiveness of God and others. He finally became able to "forgive himself." He was not off the hook for what he had done, but he had accepted that it happened and was willing to move forward without all the continuing guilt, shame, and self-hatred of the past.

Terrence says, "It took me seventeen years and sixteen days to embrace some type of forgiveness within myself for what I did to Kelly. I don't believe I'll ever fully be able to forgive myself for what I did, but on the morning after I cried in my isolation bunk as I had never cried before, I came to a sense of peace within myself. It is still an ongoing process. I look at my daughter and I can't imagine doing such a thing."

In *Embodying Forgiveness*, L. Gregory Jones writes that forgiveness is an expression of a commitment to a way of life in which people cast off their "old" selves and learn to change their relationships, seek reconciliation, and live in communion with God and with one another. This definition seems to fit Judy and Terrence perfectly and to foster a life of shalom. While they make no attempt to maintain a personal, day-to-day relationship, they have turned their backs on the anger, hate, and distrust of the past, reconciled with one another, and developed a positive, supportive relationship based on honesty, understanding, respect and acceptance, in which they wish the best for one another.

QUESTIONS FOR REFLECTION

1. Empathize with Judy and describe her feelings about Terrence at the time of the murder.
2. Describe her feelings when she met with Terrence at the Houston luncheon.
3. How do you feel that forgiveness affected Judy? Terrence?
4. Does anyone have the right or authority to forgive himself or herself for hurting others?
5. Did Judy's forgiveness help her or Terrence more?

9

SERVING OTHERS

Sitting down, He called the twelve and said to them, "If anyone wants to be first, he shall be last of all and servant of all." (Mark 9:35)

A functioning addict has been defined as a person whose drug or alcohol use hasn't caught up with them yet. This definition fit John Romaka for years—until it didn't.

John was born in Frankfurt Germany, the oldest of two sons of an army Captain father and a schoolteacher mom. When John was five, his dad left the military and the family moved to El Paso, Texas, where his father had a successful career as a broker and vice president with Merrill Lynch. John grew up in the family's nice, ranch-style house in an upper middle class suburban neighborhood and attended the Catholic Cathedral High School. He was a good student, an all-state tight end on the football team, and prominent among the popular kids. He and his friends enjoyed crossing the border to Juarez almost every weekend and taking advantage of the absence of restrictions on teenage drinking. During John's sophomore year, this became a pattern—a social thing that he felt he didn't need but was fun and the thing to do; that started small, grew over time, and escalated to include binge drinking, cocaine use, and addiction. John graduated High School and matriculated at Texas Christian University, where he says he "majored in fraternity and flunked out after a couple of years."

John returned home and attended the University of Texas at El Paso "to get his grades up," while working at various jobs, including bartending.

One night soon after his return he used so much cocaine he thought he was having a heart attack, and his parents took him to his first rehab treatment—a thirty-day, residential, twelve-step program run by the city. He says, "I went there to get my parents off my back." He finished the program, attended a local community college, and transferred to Texas Tech University, where he continued his excessive drinking, while majoring in economics and political science.

After graduation John accepted a position with Merrill Lynch in Houston. He managed his alcohol consumption, got his act together for a time, and then returned to drinking every day, using cocaine, and doing all the things he was doing before. Soon thereafter, he resigned to find less stressful work.

John found another job, married Julie, and moved to Chicago to start a new life. This post required entertaining clients, and he continued his heavy drinking, although he stopped using cocaine. After a time, he resigned from this one and accepted a sales assignment that included an expense account and required extensive travel. He did well from a business perspective, but continued to drink, missed too much work, lied about his situation, was caught drunk in a hotel, and was sent to another rehab program. About two weeks after completing the program, he was caught drinking and fired. He, Julie, and their new daughter returned to Houston.

Shortly after their return to Houston, John entered his third rehabilitation program and after completion got another good position. Julie and he divorced, he started dating Suzy, and moved to another job, where he continued to drink and behave much as in the past. He was sent by his employer for his fourth rehab. However, upon release, he was out of control and out of money, so he began stealing from Target and Walmart to support his habit. Shortly thereafter, he spent a week in the Harris County jail.

After being released from jail, John entered the Victory Family Recovery Center, funded largely by its residents' sale of banana nut bread. He spent several months selling bread as part of his fifth rehab program. When he was released from the center, he checked himself into a halfway house, and got a sponsor, a job, a company car—which he promptly wrecked—and another pink slip.

During the subsequent year-end holidays, John contacted both Julie and Suzy, by then his ex-wife and his fiancée, for help, but neither would allow him into their house. His response was a three-week bender, followed by several nights in the Harris County drunk tank. After release, he lived on alcohol and other necessities stolen from his favorites, Target and Walmart. He checked into a hospital and left against orders. He lived on the streets, panhandling to stay alive. One afternoon, he stopped at a Chevron station for a drink of water. He was so dirty, ill-kept, and threatening that the proprietor wouldn't let him inside, and instead made him drink from the spigot at the front of the station.

John finally decided, *I was raised better than this. My life shouldn't be going this way. If I continue this way, I'll end up dead. This has got to stop.*

Suzy investigated some alternatives for John and recommended he apply to enter the Salvation Army's Adult Rehabilitation Center near downtown Houston. With no reasonable alternative, John agreed. She dropped him off on the street in front of the center on a Friday morning early in 2018.

The Salvation Army is a Protestant Christian church and an international charitable organization with a worldwide membership of over 1.7 million in 133 countries, operating charity shops, shelters for the homeless, and disaster relief and humanitarian aid programs. Its purposes include the advancement of the Christian religion, the relief of poverty, and other charitable objectives beneficial to society. The Army operates Adult Rehabilitation Centers (ARC) in many cities, including five in Texas, where men and women live and participate in multi-month programs of work therapy to combat their alcohol and drug addictions.

The Houston ARC operates a residential program of work therapy, recreation, worship, health care, education, and counseling for approximately 130 men who are addicted to alcohol and drugs. It operates four family outlet stores and an associated warehouse that provide funding for the facility, rehab programs, and additional Army activities.

A couple of years before John's arrival, two people familiar with both the ARC and the Bridges To Life prison ministry reached the same conclusions: *It sure seems that most, or nearly all, incarcerated individuals struggle with alcohol and drug abuse. It also seems that a large portion of men at the Salvation Army's Houston Adult Rehabilitation Center have more than a passing acquaintance with jails or prisons. Why wouldn't Bridges To Life, designed to help people in prison, help people in the ARC equally well?*

The answer to that question led to BTL at the ARC.

The ARC will not accept anyone who is drunk. When John showed up on Friday morning, he was given a breathalyzer test, which he couldn't pass. Even after several tries throughout the day interspersed with drinking large volumes of water, he didn't sober up enough to be admitted to the program, so he began hanging out in the ARC parking lot, walking the streets, and panhandling. He walked across the street to a dog park, begged for money, and used any he received to buy alcohol at the handy Chevron station.

John quit drinking on Sunday night and was sober enough on Monday morning to be admitted at 6:00 a.m. when the center opened for admissions. He was issued clean clothes and other necessary essentials and put to work immediately, sorting rags in the warehouse.

John says:

> When I entered the ARC, I was out of resources and almost out of hope, as the reality of my situation had finally sunk in. My first day, standing in the lunch line, I was thinking, *Oh my gosh, I'm in a recovery center in the Salvation Army. What am I doing here?*
>
> It took me about thirty days to understand what was going on. I was down on myself and how my life had unraveled to the point of being in a homeless shelter for drug addicts and alcoholics. I thought my life was over and that I would lose everything—my family, my employment opportunities, my future. I resisted the help that the program offered, and I was told that unless I started applying myself, I would fail it. Then I met with a counselor who told me my problem was not that I was failing to work hard or that I was a bad person, but that I needed to get in touch with God.

People connect with God in different ways. John did so by reading the Bible, praying, attending ARC worship services, and participating in every program the ARC offered: Authentic Manhood, Men's Retreat, Bible Conference, Men's Camp, Bridges To Life, Celebrate Recovery, and AA Conflict Resolution. He says that all were helpful, and each contributed to his sobriety. However, "BTL was my favorite. I really liked the fact that people who were not employed by the ARC helped me when I was not helping myself. The confidentiality of the small groups allowed me to tell the story of my life for the first time, experience the power of telling my story, and make some great new friends. The BTL's session on forgiveness was the key. It helped me learn to forgive myself, which made it easier to ask for forgiveness from those I had harmed, and to forgive others. It showed me how to be selfless rather than selfish."

John also began to serve others through his day-to-day work. The ARC's therapy requires that all people in the program (beneficiaries) work on a regular basis in jobs connected to financing and operating the center and providing services that foster sobriety. John's first job was as a clerk in a resale store, and then he was assigned to staff the front desk at the residence building, followed by a similar job in the administrative building. After that, he worked at the weekly auction that sells donated cars and additional miscellaneous goods—and then was placed in charge of the auction. Shortly thereafter, he was assigned to manage the four resale stores that provide financing for the ARC and its activities.

John subsequently was promoted to the ARC Director of Operations, responsible for managing all aspects of the center except for client programs. He has now been a full-time Salvation Army employee for five years, and after our interview was promoted to a position managing fundraising and development for the citywide Salvation Army organization. His life had slowly but surely changed as he became a servant leader.

BECOMING A SERVANT LEADER

The term "servant leader" is of fairly modern vintage, but the concept is old, captured in Mark 10:42–45:

Jesus called them together and said, "You know that those who are regarded as rulers of the Gentiles lord it over them, and their high officials exercise authority over them. Not so with you. Instead, whoever wants to become great among you must be your servant, and whoever wants to be first must be slave of all. For even the Son of Man did not come to be served, but to serve, and to give his life as a ransom for many."

Servant leaders are both servants and leaders. Traditional leaders generally see themselves at the "top of the pyramid," and use their position to exercise power and control. Servant leaders are different. They share power and make sure others' needs and wants are honored first, causing them to grow and become happier, healthier, wiser, freer, and more fulfilled. A servant leader serves first, and then leads if appropriate. He or she strives to make sure that other people's highest priority needs are being served and that they grow as people who are more likely to become servants themselves.

Servant-leaders usually receive more from serving than they give. An example is discussed in John 2. Jesus was at a wedding and the couple was running out of wine for its guests. He told the servants to fill several big jars with water. When the water was served to the guests, it was wine! The guests never knew what happened; the servants were the ones who witnessed the miracle. The same is true today for people who serve.

Serving others is especially important for finding a strong sense of purpose and meaning in life. John first experienced this during his participation in twelve step programs in his early rehab efforts. He says, "The first three steps are the foundation of the program and after that the focus is on the renewing of the mind. The last three steps envision service to others: freely giving away what was so freely given, and helping others in their journeys to gain sobriety. Serving others is offering a hand up rather than a push down, doing what is necessary to help the next man, and in the process helping yourself. When I am serving others, I'm not thinking about drinking or doing drugs."

We've been conditioned to think of leaders as elevated above their followers, driving forward through force of will, pushing their followers to do what needs to be done. Servant leaders, however, emphasize meeting followers' needs, putting followers first, and actively tending to their personal and emotional needs. A servant leader does this by going beyond the work to be done and helping followers heal, grow, and succeed by treating them the way leaders want to be treated—which sounds very much like the "Golden Rule" of Matthew 7:12: "So in everything, do to others what you would have them do to you . . ." This rule provides a moral searchlight that reveals how to treat others and supports respect for human rights and care for the troubled and downtrodden. It teaches that we should recognize the dignity of all people, put ourselves in our neighbor's place, and guide our behavior accordingly. It is the basic principle that fosters service to others and drives servant leadership. Recognizing that the most acceptable service of God is doing good for other persons.

John continues:

> The term 'servant leadership' describes the best way for me to lead my employees and the beneficiaries dealing with their addictions—by serving them to the best of my ability and doing what is necessary to help them stay sober and live meaningful lives of service. For example, Steve checked into the center about two months after I did. I saw that he had the same desires that I had, so I placed him on a job in a store. He soon became assistant manager, then store manager, and progressed to supervisor of all stores. Another man, Sal, struggled, relapsed, left the ARC, returned, and now is doing a great job in an Austin ARC store. Many guys—clerks, truck drivers, shipping supervisors, and others have similar success stories. It is amazing to see other men having their lives changed. There is nothing more powerful than helping to change someone's life and the way to do that is to serve them—to be there when they need you. For me, doing that has become a calling and not a job. I have seen so many miracles happen.

Organizations, like individuals, become servant leaders when the institutions themselves exist to serve people and society and mediate care for persons who serve each other. Servant organizations have an identity, value system, and capabilities that foster love and purpose, whereas self-serving organizations aim to protect their own interests, even at the detriment of people they claim to serve. The leaders in servant organizations apply servant leadership practices to empower and activate individual talent and potential to achieve a higher purpose. They create organizational cultures that enhance the engagement levels of the people they serve.

The Salvation Army Adult Rehabilitation Center and Bridges To Life are examples of servant leader organizations, as each helps suffering people change for the better and begin to break cycles of misery and brokenness. Like throwing a stone into a still pond—the stone hits the water in one place, but its effects move out in a circle and affect the water in many places—the organizations have a "ripple effect" for good, as they help break the cycle of addiction and misbehavior for participants, and also for their families, in the present and in the future. John says, "The Salvation Army not only helped me. It helped my family, my kids, and their kids. The best thing that's happened to me in my recovery is the restoration of my family. My brother and I were estranged but now are best friends. We talk every day. Through dementia and Alzheimer's my dad never forgot that I was sober. My mom tells me all the time that she doesn't know how we would have made it if I hadn't gotten sober. I have wonderful relationships with my two children."

Serving others, whether as an individual or as a leader, often is a complex undertaking that plays out in different ways under different circumstances and requires different mindsets and talents. The mindset that underlies them all is humility.

PRACTICE HUMILITY

Trying to explain humility is a humbling experience that somehow seems unhumble and immodest. A humble person, it seems, must be unaware of their own humility. If you have it, you won't know it; and if you believe you have it, you probably don't. Without any claim of being an expert on the subject, I will share some learnings from John and others that hopefully will help you think more deeply about humility and its importance to serving others.

Humility has been defined by different people in various ways. John describes it as "understanding that everything I have was given to me by a God of mercy and grace, and it can be lost by going back into my ego and self."

A more detailed view is that humility is the ability to view one's self accurately as an individual with flaws as well as talents, while not being arrogant or having low self-esteem. Humility is an attitude of spiritual modesty that comes from understanding our place in the larger order of things, not taking our desires, successes, or failings too seriously, and respecting other people. C.S. Lewis, in *Mere Christianity*, described humility as "not to think less of oneself but to think of oneself less."[13] Humility accepts self but is not self-focused or self-centered. It is the opposite of pride, arrogance, and an inflated sense of our importance and talents, but it has nothing to do with meekness or weakness, or with being self-effacing or submissive. Humility envisions a fundamentally caring and compassionate attitude toward others and caring for what they have to offer. Psychological studies have indicated that humility fosters positive behavior and enhances our ability to learn and be effective leaders.

Leaders often do not see the true value of the people they are leading, especially when those people are addicted to alcohol and drugs. But when leaders have the humility to admit that they can benefit from the contribution of others who have less power and fewer accomplishments, and show them respect and actively seek their ideas and unique contributions, the outcomes can be of real value. This was the case in John's management of the ARC's businesses, which under his leadership saw dramatic cultural improvement, major productivity increases, and a doubling of store sales revenue. John demonstrated the paradox of power that is seen in servant leadership: he gained power by giving it to the weak. He served recovering addicts through practices that advance their interests and empowered them to improve their contributions, such as empathy, collaboration, open mindedness, fairness, generosity, and trust. This conveyed a sense of humility that helped them feel affirmed, appreciated, encouraged, and validated, and they responded by contributing beyond anyone's expectations.

Understanding the meaning of humility, admiring it from a distance, and talking about it are not enough. We all need to restrain our pride and cultivate humility by engaging in the purposeful application of principles and practices that foster it. Each person needs to develop their own strategy for doing so. A conversation between puritan clergyman Cotton Mather (1663–1728) and young Benjamin Franklin (1706–1790) presents an interesting example. Franklin was visiting in Mather's home and was walking on a narrow staircase with a low ceiling. Mather yelled, "stoop!" Franklin, not responding quickly enough, hit his head on a beam. Mather reacted, "let this be a caution to you not always to hold your head so high. Stoop, young man, stoop, as you go through the world and you'll miss many hard thumps."

Outlined below are some thoughts from John's experience, from my reading, study, and experience, and significantly from *Humility: True Greatness* by C. J. Mahaney.

Humility starts with our attitude—our way of thinking or feeling about ourselves and others as reflected in our behavior. It is a choice we make of our free will regarding how we hold ourselves out toward God and the people around us. A person with a humble attitude submits to the authority of God; accepts their own weaknesses, vulnerability, and limitations; is not pretentious and ambitious; thinks not of their place in society but listens to and serves others; and honestly evaluates self and is open to correction and critique. No matter how great their accomplishments or positive characteristics may be, they do not expect special treatment.

James 4:6–7 reads: "God opposes the proud but shows favor to the humble. Submit yourselves, then, to God." Jesus is the ultimate example of humility. He did not act as a God. Instead, He came in the likeness of men and took on the form of a servant. He did not value His own self-importance or honor, but freely suffered so that God's will could be carried out and God could be glorified through His life.

To be humble is to have the same mindset. Your posture before God should be a complete submission to his wise providence in your life, with a firm confidence that what He does is for your good. Acknowledging your need for God involves controlling your thoughts and speaking truth to yourself rather than listening to lies from yourself. You can declare war on pride and affirm your dependence on God and your need for him by practicing spiritual disciplines such as the following:

- Remember that God has forgiven you and others.
- Read the Bible and apply it to your life.
- Routinely confess your sins and repent as appropriate.
- "Pray continually," sharing your joys, fears, goals, desires, and failures, thanking Him for His blessings, and asking for His help.
- Wait patiently for Him to act.

John expresses his faith and need for God this way:

> I am a firm believer in Divine intervention. We all have a choice—either God is everything or he is nothing. If he is everything, then everything in my life is the way it should be. This takes me out of the equation. When I help others like I'm supposed to, God handles the rest. I have problems in my life like we all do, but not one of them shakes my reliance on God or my ability to stay sober. Somewhere along the way I had lost contact with God, but when I entered the ARC, I re-established the relationship. My purpose is to ensure that every man that comes through its door has the same experience. I believe I had to go through all the things I went through to be where I am today.

Humility is worked into our lives through service, particularly anonymous service, to others. We are not called to servanthood primarily because others need our service, but because of what happens to us when we serve. Serving others disciplines our focus on self and transforms us. When we serve others, a deep change occurs in us. We are happier, feel a warm glow in our being, have higher self-esteem, and feel a sense of empowerment, purpose, and fulfillment. Helping others gives us a front-row seat to witness their hardships, which can help us feel humble about our own circumstances and practice gratitude.

The pursuit of humility nearly always requires help, as we can rarely deal with our pride and arrogance alone. Pride affects our self-perception which is rarely accurate. Others usually can see us better than we can see ourselves, and they have insights into our souls that we cannot see. Without help, we will listen to our own arguments, believe our own lies, and cater to our own delusions. Others can impart clarity that helps protect us from ourselves and receive God's grace, so we need to encourage others to invite themselves into our lives, and graciously receive correction and seek constructive feedback. As noted in Proverbs 12: 15, "The way of fools seems right to them, but the wise listen to advice."

Golf is a wonderful metaphor that has taught me a great deal about humility. It starts with so many opportunities for excessive pride and arrogance. Think about it. You arrive at a plush country club decked out in Ralph Lauren's RLX Golf attire—are met by an attendant who delivers your bag of Callaway clubs to a caddy who caters to your every need and announces "great shot" for every swing except a whiff—and you revel in congratulatory lies in the nineteenth hole.

However, if you've ever played golf, you recognize the humiliating reality for nearly all players: duffs, dribblers, hooks, slices, worm burners, and sometimes mulligans and foot wedges. I know. I've been there. For nearly all of us, a round of golf is a lesson in humility. We rarely are as good as we look or think we are. And that's all too common in other parts of our lives. All too frequently we duff a shot and act like it is a hole in one. A little more humility would probably help in our service of others and in developing relationships with them.

QUESTIONS FOR REFLECTION

1. Do you have any addictions? (Thinking more broadly than drugs and alcohol.)
2. What role did hope play in John Romaka's life?
3. The attendant at the Chevron station wouldn't let John inside and instead made him drink from the spigot at the front of the station. How did this affect John?

4. What characteristic do you believe is most important for a servant leader?
5. What spiritual disciplines make you more humble?

10

Maintaining Good Relationships

Live in harmony with one another. Do not be proud, but be willing to associate with people of low position. Do not be conceited. Do not repay anyone evil for evil. Be careful to do what is right in the eyes of everyone. If it is possible, as far as it depends on you, live at peace with everyone. (Romans 12:16–18)

Maintaining good relationships with other people is a key element in finding shalom. In Chapter 6, I cited Viktor Frankl for the proposition that there are some things, like happiness, that you should not aim for or target, as they cannot be effectively pursued. Instead, they only happen as the consequence of your dedication to another cause. It seems to me that building good relationships is one of those situations. I don't believe you can effectively pursue a relationship as such, but you can do many things from which a good relationship is likely to ensue.

A relationship is a connection between people. You can have relationships—good ones or bad ones—with a wide range of people. The phrase "being in a relationship," while often linked with romance, can refer to various connections such as family, friends, business associates, or even strangers with common interests.

The Bible is a roadmap for dealing with others and building relationships. As discussed in Chapter 7, the Ten Commandments, the Sermon on the Mount, and the commandment to love one another all foster relationships that are right, positive, and good; and that are maintained with honesty, integrity, and straightforwardness—not just an absence of conflict or tolerance of one another. Such connections do not just happen. They have to be developed.

DEVELOPING RELATIONSHIPS

You are a social creature, and relationships are at the very core of your existence. Your connection with other humans began at birth. You don't need all of them all the time, but relationships continue to be important, many for all of your life. Family members usually are caregivers, so interwoven and interdependent that some say it's almost like you live under the same "emotional skin." Peers and friends contribute to your psychological development, teach you about emotional states of other people, and often help provide for your needs and wants, such as security, trust, and intimacy. Colleagues affect your work status and satisfaction.

The everyday stresses of life often make relationships difficult to build and challenging to maintain, and sometimes they falter or break; and sometimes they are fixed and falter or break again. And again. You need relationships though, either to maintain connection with specific individuals or to preserve a core group of relationships that help you over time. You often need to work to do those things from which a relationship is likely to ensue and keep working to "put Humpty Dumpty together again," when a connection falters or breaks. When relations faulter or break with God or others, you need to restore peace by mending relationships that have broken. And you need to build on and maintain relationships with God and others, which is key to a lifetime of shalom.

Chaos and skewed family relationships often create opposition to shalom. Crystal Daniel is an example. She grew up in Hillsboro. Texas, the second oldest of three sisters and one brother. Her mom was a Christian woman who took the children to church regularly and instilled God in their lives on a daily basis. But her father was addicted to drugs and alcohol and was abusive, frequently beating her mom. He was so bad that Crystal prayed to God that He would take her father away. She says:

I hated my father. I remember asking God to just let him die—then we found out he had a brain tumor. According to his doctor, he had the second largest type of brain tumor, called Astrocytoma, caused by all the drug use. He died when I was fifteen. I was amazed at how Mom stuck with him during his sickness.

After he got sick, Dad asked us kids if he could go to church camp with us. We agreed, and he attended even though he was in bad shape. We were at a tent revival and he walked up on the stage and took a microphone from the pastor and admitted to all of us what he had done to us and asked for our forgiveness. Tears of joy flowed like a river down our cheeks. It was all we could ever have hoped for. That night I told him I forgave him. It was beautiful. The pastor came down, unified us as a family, and prayed us into forgiveness. I will never forget that night.

It was a bittersweet ending. We had about seven good months with him as a father from the time he was diagnosed until he died. Outside of the drugs, alcohol, and abuse Dad was an amazing person. He started to show us love. He was a decent man who had problems and we learned to love him. We prayed for a miracle, that he would live, but it didn't happen. The slow, agonizing way he died was too much. After he died, I just couldn't take it anymore. I was traumatized by my life and Dad's death. I was grieving and didn't know how to process it. I turned to rebellion, alcohol, drugs, and the streets at fifteen. My life was never the same.

Crystal developed some interesting "relationships" on the streets: with people she sold drugs to, bought drugs from, did drugs with, partied with, got high with, committed crimes with. They were common on the path she was on, headed to destruction with no plan and no purpose. She describes her connections this way: "Our relationships were not relationships. They were 'associates.' They were the people that I ran with and dealt with on the streets, who are not in my life today. There was no true relationship whatsoever."

She continued, "I had a relationship with my family until I burned my bridges and they told me not to come around anymore. I burned bridges by stealing from them, lying to them, getting money from them by claiming I was hungry and using the money for drugs, and doing all the things that crack addicts do. Drugs became me, and all I thought about was that next hit."

Crystal was arrested for public intoxication when she was eighteen years old. Subsequent to that, she was arrested thirty-two times for crimes such as criminal mischief, trespass, possession of marijuana, forgery, theft, and burglary. She served eight prison sentences; and was assigned to twelve rehabilitation centers.

When Crystal was in prison, she stayed to herself as much as she could, but she did have two "bunkees" that she still has a good relationship with today. She says:

> I don't know what I would have done if I had not met them. I lived in a dorm with about 120 women. We were assigned to bottom and top bunks. I had some pretty rough bunkees at times. But two times I was paired with heaven-sent women. We leaned on each other and prayed ourselves through our difficulties together. You're in such a small space that you have to form a bond. You have to make it work or you end up fighting your way through prison, which was something I didn't want to do. You can tell the difference between a real and a false relationship, and ours was real.

Sometime events occur that provide fresh starts. They prompt you to behave differently, and you feel compelled to change yourself and your circumstances. That happened to Crystal when she was pregnant and spent the entire nine months of her pregnancy in jail. The day of labor, she was transferred by a Deputy Sheriff to a local hospital. Her mom was there. When her daughter was born, Crystal was allowed to hold her for only twenty minutes before releasing her to her mother for foster care. She explained, "What got me was that I was only able to hold her for twenty minutes. That set the tone for me. I went back to prison and my normal life. That's all I knew, but it really hurt me when I couldn't go with my baby. I told myself and God, *do whatever it takes but I've got to change my life.*

I began to change from that moment on. I also graduated from the Bridges To Life program, which greatly helped with my change."

Crystal was released on parole in 2008 and assigned to a Salvation Army transitional facility in Dallas for ninety days. She then found a job as a waitress at IHOP, where she worked for five years until she resigned to return to school full time. Crystal earned three associate degrees, a Bachelor's in Diverse Studies, and a master's degree in social work from the University of Texas at Arlington, specializing in advanced community practice. She reestablished her relationship with her family and had her children returned to her from foster care. She was released from parole in 2019.

Crystal worked for a time at a local non-profit and then in March of 2023 co-founded and became CEO of B.A.N.E. (Building and Empire) Institute, a not-for-profit organization that aims to empower women re-entering society after incarceration by providing post and prerelease peer-to-peer counseling, case management services, and other life changing resources that transform the lives of women. She continues to serve there today, helping transform women whose lives are like hers was.

MAINTAINING RELATIONSHIPS

Living in right relationship with one another and with God, the way in which "shalom" is used that is closest to the way "peace" is usually used, contemplates good, regulated, normal relationships between nations, groups, or individuals or between individuals and God. Such relationships are right, positive, and good—not just an absence of conflict or tolerating one another; and are maintained in the face of physical separation and alienation,

For most people, relationships with other people are either an essential feature of health, well-being and peace, or a central contributor to discomfort and conflict. Relationships improve or deteriorate but rarely stay the same. They are at the core of the personal change process. Myriad changes occur, such as openness to various experiences, new values, different modes of power. Crystal's relationships changed dramatically over the years from what they were with her dysfunctional family, during her life of crime, her time in prison, her immediate post release days, to what they are now.

She credits her relationships with others—family, law enforcement mentors, work colleagues, alcohol and drug recovery sponsors, and friends—for much of her success:

> I strongly believe that the people God has placed in my life are here to stay. I have a circle of friends whom I am so grateful for that I look up to. I take their suggestions and guidance in consideration because I know they truly care about me and what I care about. God has given me the opportunity to meet and have close connections with people that want to see me win and have a heart to serve God, they help me and mentor me along my way. I would have never thought in a million years that my circle would be made up of the individuals they are. God has favored me, washed me clean, restored my life and I would never take that for granted. I could have been dead a thousand times over and God saved my life. I believe that it was the grace of God that I'm not serving a life sentence today. I look back and see miracles all around me and the hedge of protection that secured my safety.

One can speculate as to why and how Crystal was able to make such change in her life, from the life of a criminal to the life of a God fearing, contributing member of society intent on compensating for the harm she caused to others. I suspect there were many factors, but the main one had to do with change in Crystal's way of being and her beginning to care about and work for peace with others.

In *Anatomy of Peace: Resolving the Heart Conflict*, the Arbinger Institute, an organization that focuses on conflict management, presents the case that there is something deeper than our behavior, something they call our "way of being," that is inextricably tied to the way we see and regard people. People all live in being with others, and there are basically two ways of doing so: people can see others as objects, or they can see others as people. If people see others as objects they see them as obstacles, vehicles, irrelevancies, or nothings of no more value than an empty vase on a table. They will get to the point where they see each other as disagreeable rather than as simply disagreeing, and end up provoking each other and causing conflict rather than dealing with it.

We need, instead, to see others as people. Arbinger suggests that you assess how you regard other people by considering your relationships and asking yourself this question: "Do my relationships with people who look like me—in skin color, gender, sexual orientation, age, religious views, or physical ability—seem different in quality than those with people who don't look like me in any of these ways?"[14] If you have a different level of relationship with those who look like you versus those who don't, ask yourself why. The answer may be that you are viewing them as objects.

Crystal was seen as an object, and saw others as objects, in years past. Her dad treated her as an object at best, and sometimes seemed not to recognize her existence. She saw the victims of her crimes as objects—personal irrelevancies she was trying to get her next fix from, and not human beings she was hurting. She never developed relationships with them.

But Crystal changed, and came to see others as people: individual persons with free will and a conscience, the capacity to know God and be guided by a higher moral order, with hopes, cares, fears, and needs of their own. So, she quit using and exploiting others and began to serve them. She co-founded the B.A.N.E. Institute, to help women whose lives had been like hers transform their lives and relationships; and in so doing see themselves and be seen as people rather than objects. Crystal's experience models shalom for all of us.

Healthy relationships are best described as interdependent. Interdependence means you rely on each other for mutual support but still maintain your identity as a unique individual. Your relationship is balanced. You know you have the other's approval and love, but your self-esteem doesn't depend on them. Although you're there for each other, you don't depend on each other to get all of your needs met.

Healthy relationships don't just happen. People come together for many different reasons, and every relationship is unique. Connections are built, often over a long period of time and with great effort, and each relationship is different, depending on the people involved. There is no "one-fits-all," magic formula. However, if you want to build or improve your relationships with others, consider the following.

See People as People

You and others—friends, family, and even strangers—are people and not objects, and should be treated accordingly. To foster a healthy relationship, you need to see people as being in authentic, inclusive, and resilient relationships where individuals are interconnected, share responsibility towards one another, and experience belonging, support, and mutual care. You also should seek peace and harmony, create an environment where love and understanding can flourish, and foster an atmosphere of unity and reconciliation. Don't just contribute to your own well-being, but also inspire a ripple effect of peace and harmony within your community. Think about the difference in the way Crystal's dad connected to her before and after his sickness was diagnosed. He changed his approach from ignoring her or seeing her as an object, to treating her as a human being who was his daughter. And that began the change in their relationship.

Be Fully Present.

We often get so caught up in the nitty-gritty of daily life that we forget to be present with others. And sometimes there are events in our life that need much of our time and effort. As discussed in more detail in Chapter 3, to demonstrate love and maintain relationships, we need to be fully present and practice presence on an ongoing basis. We need to check in periodically and talk to each other beyond the routine niceties. Being truly present in another person's life means involving yourself in their hopes and dreams and taking time to notice and compliment their accomplishments. It also involves showing genuine empathy when they are facing challenges.

Demonstrate Respect

Demonstrating respect starts with respecting yourself. Self-respect is often defined as a sense of worth or as due respect for oneself. It includes self-esteem, self-confidence, dignity, self-love, a sense of honor, self-reliance, and pride. It is the opposite of shame, putting one's self down, arrogance, and self-importance. Self-respect includes being strong enough to admit when you're wrong and apologize without feeling threatened, and also the confidence to allow people to be themselves without being controlled by you. If you have low self-respect, your confidence in others is also low, making it difficult to develop relationships with others because of your difficulty in handling the consequences if they don't deliver on your expectations. On the other hand, higher self-respect means you can trust others because you are willing and able to handle the consequences if they should break your trust. In summary, having the self-respect to trust yourself helps you trust others.

Respect is most often considered to involve how you see the other person rather than how you see yourself. Respect means treating another as you would want to be treated. You treat them as individual persons, and attempt to understand their values, aspirations, and beliefs. You let them know that they have priority, encourage them, affirm their value, and express sincere appreciation for them as valuable human beings. One of the most important ways of showing another person respect is to meet their needs and acknowledge their value without putting them down. Never belittle or look at them with condescension or contempt. Remember that every time you treat another in a way that breaches a basic level of respect, you will damage the relationship you have—and if you treat them with respect, you will build it.

Maintain Boundaries

Personal boundaries are typically unstated guidelines or rules that people set to place limits on how other people behave toward them. They may include physical, mental, emotional, and spiritual boundaries. Healthy boundaries define what is appropriate behavior in your relationships. They create mutual respect between individuals, help them know what's expected, and show them how they can respect each other's personal space, comfort level, and limits. They differ from person to person and are determined by variations in culture, personality, and social context. For example, boundaries appropriate in a business setting would seem irrelevant in a dinner with old friends.

Setting boundaries defines our expectations of ourselves and others in different kinds of relationships. Without boundaries, relationships can easily become breeding grounds for codependency, resentment, control dynamics, and the erosion of emotional intimacy. The boundaries Crystal's family set during the time of her bad behavior no doubt avoided some of these issues and helped preserve the relationship for the long-term. When people care to understand, communicate, and honor each other's boundaries consistently, relationships can thrive.

Think about what is important day-to-day and what will matter most when you look back on your life. It's probably not work, money, status, or other such considerations. It's the care and connection you share with your friends, family, and co-workers. Healthy relationships sow the seeds of well-being, and well-being strengthens your relationships for now and the future. To create such relationships, you might need to change yourself.

QUESTIONS FOR REFLECTION

1. What factors are most important to you for a good relationship?
2. Describe your best and worst personal relationships.
3. What is the main difference between the two relationships and why does that difference exist?
4. Do you view people as objects or as people?
5. Which of the factors discussed is most important to you in building and maintaining relationships?

11

CHANGING YOUR LIFE

I can do all things through him who strengthens me. (Philippians 4:13)

T he story of Joseph in the book of Genesis is a powerful story of change that reminds us that difficult circumstances can be a setting for incredible change. Joseph's jealous brothers threw him into a pit to get rid of him. A short while later, they spotted a caravan passing the scene, and the brothers sold Joseph to the traders. He was eventually taken to Egypt, where he was sold to Potiphar, one of King Pharaoh's ministers, and thrown into prison for a crime he did not commit. His remarkable ability to interpret dreams caught the attention of Pharaoh, the ruler of Egypt, who was troubled by a perplexing dream; and Joseph was freed and rose to become a powerful ruler in Egypt, second in command only to Pharaoh. He saved his family and the entire nation from famine, and in so doing became a model for transformational change.

We all face an unsettling amount of change in our lives as evidenced by the alarming frequency of job changes, relocations, marriages, births, divorces, health problems, drug abuse, incarcerations, retirements, family strife, and other shifts in us as individuals and in society. This magnitude of change can prompt a gloomy vision, or it can be seen as an opportunity for a fundamental shift in how we define ourselves, where we are going, and how we will get there.

I recommend that change in circumstances, good or bad, be viewed as an opportunity. By better managing change that is thrust upon you or that you initiate, you can make a difference in the course of events affecting you, your family and friends, and your community, and in so doing foster shalom in your life

The purpose of this book has been to present ideas that will help readers change their lives to ones that are presenting a better understanding of shalom along with ideas and examples of how different people have found it in their lives. These examples, like Judy's forgiveness that was fostered by men in her BTL small groups, and Eddie's hopes that felt impossible until he attended the church services in prison, demonstrate that shalom doesn't happen on its own. Rather, shalom ensues when you do the hardest work, engage in the most struggles, tell the most demanding truth, and make the most needed changes. The preceding chapters outlined several behavior patterns that when pursued tend to foster shalom. Improving performance in each area requires, in nearly all cases, personal transformation. The following is intended to provide some guidance in making such change in your life.

Changes can be of three types or levels. Macro changes, such as changes in world leaders, attitudes toward the climate, or a country's economic policy, are changes that affect you as part of the larger world you live in. Organizational changes are those that occur within institutions that affect your life, such as new requirements at a school you attend or layoffs where you work. Micro changes involve and directly affect you, your spouse, family, or close friends and associates. "I" change when they occur.

Some micro changes are forced upon you, like if you are laid off from a job, lose a parent or child, or suffer another type of trauma. You initiate other micro changes, such as when you intentionally change jobs, move from an apartment to a house, or get married. *Finding Shalom* mainly considers micro changes that you make or need to make—primarily involving moves from a status quo that is less than desirable to one that is more desirable and may include a life of shalom.

Nearly all people seeking to improve their lives experience challenges and difficult circumstances, and some face tragedy, suffering, and despair. Many of the people discussed in the preceding chapters changed from a criminal life or a life of addiction, through a transition involving prison or rehab, to a more complete and fulfilling life. Most of them became law-abiding citizens who improved their lives and are seeking to make them even better. Others have confronted troubles and misfortunes, dealt with them as best they could, and still are seeking lives of wholeness and tranquility. All want a state of shalom, and they will need to initiate and carry out change to find it.

The problem is, there commonly are forces resisting change to the status quo: forces like addictions, peer pressure, cultural issues, loneliness, arrogance, ego, and other issues that make it easier for you to continue your life as it has been.

For change to occur, your drive for a different life (such as the desire to avoid another incarceration, empathy with those affected, want of a fulfilling life, belief in religious teachings, and others) must become stronger than and overcome the forces resisting the change. For this to happen, you need to understand your dissatisfaction with the current state as well as the opportunities for improving it.

Change of a type that can lead from a troubled life to a life of shalom is nearly always more than just thinking and behaving differently. Instead, it is a radical and deliberate change in heart, attitude, and behavior in which your fundamental character and being become permanently different. It is a transformation of your beliefs, behaviors, and perspectives to become the best version of yourself. It is repentance.

Repentance is difficult and often not an easy process. C. S. Lewis, in *Mere Christianity*, described it as follows:

> In other words, fallen man is not simply an imperfect creature who needs improvements: he is a rebel who must lay down his arms. Laying down your arms, surrendering, saying you are sorry, realizing that you have been on the wrong track and getting ready to start life over again from the ground floor—that is the only way out of our "hole". This process of surrender—this movement full speed astern—is what Christians call repentance. Now repentance is no fun at all. It is something much harder than merely eating humble pie. It means

unlearning all the self-conceit and self-will that we have been train-
ing ourselves into for thousands of years. It means killing part of
yourself, undergoing a kind of death.[15]

Personal transformation empowers you to break free from limitations,
embrace new opportunities, and reach your full potential. It is a little like
climbing a mountain. When you reach the top, you are in an entirely new
world that is very different from where you started. The old world is still
there, but it is less significant, and you see it differently. When you enter
your new world, you have experienced a transformation. It usually is a
difficult struggle, with temptations to quit and turn back. The first step is
to be sure there is good reason for making the journey.

NEED FOR CHANGE

The process of personal change usually is viewed differently by different
people, and each situation requires a different journey. Volumes have
been written addressing change processes, and a short chapter in a short
book will not come close to covering the subject. However, most paths of
change include some common elements and start with being clear about
the need for change. To do this, you first need to assess where you are.

Understand your Current State

John Steinbeck, one of my favorite writers, once said, "to find where you
are going, you must know where you are." So it is with change. Your life
may reach an equilibrium—a status quo that is unlikely to change unless
you do something about it. This status quo is the starting point. Assessing it can help you understand the cost or pain of changing, or of not
changing. Dissatisfaction with your status quo can motivate you to seek to
change it and illuminate opportunities for doing so. Seeking improvement
in your status quo can provide a goal, or target, for change.

Assessing your life can be a challenge, and depending on the circumstances, may require professional help. However, you can evaluate
different areas of your life and know whether you are satisfied with it.
Such areas might include career, relationships, health, finances, personal

growth, and more. By assessing such areas, you can gain a clearer picture of how well-balanced your life is as a jumping off point to a new status quo that you may need to change to.

Self-appraisal is a conscious assessment of your goals, your behavior, your relationships, and other significant domains of your life. It allows you to expand your options, have a deeper life experience, learn, and come clean with your errors. Assessing yourself might include consideration of issues such as:

- How you spend your time and with whom.
- The quality of the time you spend with others.
- Other choices you make about yourself, such as how you eat and how you drink.
- Your performance in general and your performance toward your goals.

It is important to assess your situation, behaviors, and traits honestly—but not rate your inherent worthiness as a human being. It is more helpful to focus on corrections rather than failings and to try to set the starting point for identifying a new path for your life.

Describe a New State

One wanting to change needs to draw a mental picture of what life will look like after the change and focus on the direction this leads them. Decisions concerning a new status should be from both the head (appeals to logic, data and reason) and the heart (appeals to how you feel and what you want). Putting hard data behind your decisions is smart, but most effective change also requires you to dig a little deeper and feel good about your decision. St. Ignatius' discernment process, discussed in Chapter 2, will help you meet this need.

Most changes affect many people: spouses, family, friends, often the community at large. Many of them will have to adjust their day-to-day activities to accommodate your change, and often some will need to be involved in every stage of a change process—from identifying challenges and planning the new status quo to implementation and reflection. Their participation will help them understand the reasoning behind the change, be invested in it, and contribute to the implementation.

Change

Once you are clear about where you are and what you want your new status to be, it's time to change. The process is a little like retraining a horse. If you ride a horse through the same path every time, it will only reluctantly go down a new path, and it will hesitate every time it gets to a juncture. It's only by consistently guiding the horse down a different path that you can help it unlearn the old and learn the new. Similarly, in change you have to adopt different paths, and unlearn the old and learn the new. And the learning begins with picking the best time to start.

Pick Your Time

Timing is important to change. Events, some systemic and predictable and others not, often occur and provide fresh starts that prompt you to behave differently, and you feel compelled to change yourself and your circumstances. Some of the events are large and some are small. For example, most of the individuals mentioned in this book experienced fresh starts when they were released from prison or got a job—rather significant life events. Others have experienced fresh starts and incentives to change from smaller occurrences or events of synchronicity, like Debbie hearing the voice in the back seat of her car, or a near miss of an auto accident, increased rental cost of an apartment, or failing a college course. Regardless of the significance of the event, these are moments when the labels you use to describe yourself shift, (say from "inmate" to "job applicant") and can become the start of a new life chapter and a clean slate for change. New starts occurred, for example, when Charles was offered a job with BTL, when small group members asked Judy about forgiving Terrence, when John was so dirty and disheveled that he was required to drink from a water spigot, and when Crystal was only allowed to hold her newborn daughter for twenty minutes after her birth.

If your life needs a change toward one that will foster shalom, think about what will give you a fresh start. Recognizing and highlighting opportunities to create fresh starts, even if they're small, like the start of a new week, can change behavior. Some fresh start events just happen while others might be planned by you. Whether they are accidental or serendipitous, significant true events or just impressions such as New Year's Day or your birthday, a fresh start event should motivate you to behave differently, help you disrupt bad habits, and provide a clean slate not burdened by the baggage of the past. It should not be so much a new chapter in your life story, but rather a new book about a different you. A good example is Crystal, whose fresh start was provided by the birth of her daughter in jail and only being able to spend twenty minutes with her newborn before going back to her cell, combined with participation in BTL in prison.

Set Goals

Now—your challenge is doing it! What do you do to actually change? This is not an easy question. You need to be discerning in answering it, and setting goals is a great way to do this. Goal setting is a powerful process for thinking about your future, and for motivating you to do what is appropriate to make it the best it can be. The process helps you choose where you want to go in life and where to concentrate your efforts. Setting goals allows you to plan your life and feel a sense of accomplishment and self-worth when you have succeeded.

Processes for using goals can vary, and a number of websites contain good information about establishing and using them. A powerful, commonly used approach is the use of SMART goals—written goals and objectives that are:

S—Specific
M—Measurable
A—Attainable
R—Relevant
T—Time-bound/Trackable

This approach involves setting a very few overarching goals that are broad in scope and almost aspirational, supported by several more limited objectives that, if accomplished, will fulfill the goals. You may wish to set goals and objectives in a number of areas of your life, such as career, financial, or others, from which shalom is likely to ensue. If you feel ready to begin preparation or action, consider whether your goals and plans are realistic. Consider what, where, when, and how things will be done. Think about specific steps you will you take, what the potential obstacles are, and what you will do if things don't go as planned?

Seek Support

Consider asking a loved one, friend, colleague, or professional to help you achieve your goals. Such social connections can provide support in various ways when you are dealing with changes in your life. People can listen and provide empathy, encouragement, and comfort. Social connections can also be a great way to learn things and gain information that you might need as you make a change. And sometimes, changes bring a need for actual physical help with certain tasks. Whatever the case, lean on your support network.

Go Slow to Change Fast

Lasting change often happens slowly over time. Trying to rush the process can lead to mistakes and often result in going to an extreme, burning out, and having the pendulum swing to the other extreme. Let change happen at a pace that feels right to you, but remember that taking the time to do the right things the right way is likely to speed up the process.

If you're looking to change one area in your life, keep it to one area. Trying to change many things all at once can be a setup for exhaustion and defeat. You can often break a needed change into small, more attainable goals. Slow and gradual modification, rather than huge abrupt change, gives you the opportunity to take things one step at a time, which can be more productive and more likely to result in permanent change.

Manage Resistance

Resistance to change refers to the substantive, psychological, or emotional barriers that individuals experience when confronted with the need to adapt or modify their established beliefs, behaviors, or routines.

Substantive barriers are actual circumstances that prevent one from changing. For example, some changes might be prevented by addiction or other illnesses, and sometimes people do not have the financial resources to make short-term changes that would be to their advantage in the long term. Deeply held beliefs might prevent certain changes. Sometimes ego is the culprit, and the hubris of believing in absolutes or thinking they are always right causes people to stay the way they are.

A key to the problem is to understand that resistance is usually not to the actual change, but to related social change—the change in human relationships that generally accompanies substantive change. Resistance is usually created because of certain blind spots and attitudes you have about yourself and the world—a function of how you think and the habits that guide you. Some more common such reasons for resistance are:

- Attachment to the status quo: When you have grown accustomed to certain routines or ways of thinking, you may resist change simply because you feel comfortable and secure in your current state. Sometimes it's more comfortable to have things stay the same because you know what to expect. Or you might be unwilling to change when "everyone else" is staying the same and peer pressure rules. Or perhaps you procrastinate and just put off or delay change that you know needs to happen, or you just are lazy for a time. Remember that when you stick with what you have, you miss the opportunity of experiencing something better.

- Loss of control: Change can disrupt familiar routines and dynamics, leading to a loss of perceived control. You may resist change because you fear relinquishing your sense of autonomy or influence over your circumstances. Sometimes pushing back on changes ends up hurting you more. When you hold on to control at all costs, your attempts to control change end up controlling you. You can practice letting go by imagining yourself welcoming change with open hands and a willing heart.

- Fear of the unknown: Change often brings unfamiliarity and potential risks, which can trigger anxiety and fear and make you hesitant to step out of your comfort zone. You can best deal with the fear and anxiety by staying in the present. You don't know what will happen next, but can you handle what is happening now? Deal with the situation you are in, not the next one that might be coming. This may involve identifying and examining the specific fears associated with the change, understanding their underlying causes, and challenging their validity. By reframing fear as an opportunity for growth and viewing uncertainty as a natural part of the change process, you can gradually reduce the resistance.

- Perception that the pain will exceed the gain: Change often requires you to invest time, energy, and effort into new situations. The perceived burden creates resistance, especially if the benefits of change are not clearly understood or valued. Change is uncomfortable and takes energy to adapt and mental effort to learn new things. Carefully consider the pros and cons of each planned change and do not assume that the pain exceeds the gain. Consider the change as a form of learning and growth and remember that growing pains can feel good when you lean into them and embrace them. You can feel the pain of change and enjoy making progress toward your values and learning from your mistakes.

In summary, more often than not you need to deal with resistance and go forward with change by first dealing with yourself and changing your beliefs and attitudes. The first step in overcoming resistance is to recognize and acknowledge the need for change. Engaging in honest self-reflection allows you to identify areas of your life that could benefit from transformation. A deep examination of personal beliefs and values, as well as current circumstances, behaviors, and outcomes will help you recognize any patterns or areas that are no longer serving your growth or well-being and need to be changed to help you find shalom.

QUESTIONS FOR REFLECTION

1. What changes do you need to make in your life?
2. What are some fresh start events in your life?
3. What personal resistors have most commonly caused you to resist needed change?
4. Discuss some cases where your beliefs and attitudes caused you to resist change. How did you deal with them?
5. Who will support you when you need a change?
6. What is one overarching goal in your life that would require you to change?

CONCLUSION

Most of us don't have overwhelming or incapacitating problems in our lives, but we still yearn for more. We yearn for a life of shalom—a life that is complete, perfect, and full in mind, body and soul. If you are yearning for a better, more complete life, implementing the ideas presented in *Finding Shalom: Journeys Beyond Peace* should help you find it. It has not presented shalom as a stand-alone target. Instead, it has related the stories of several BTL participants and other individuals to describe a number of beliefs and actions that tend to have side-effects that foster shalom.

Shalom is more than a way of living. It is a way of harmonizing the spirit, the soul, the body, and the mind. Shalom is about the voice and spirit of God permeating your life. It's about believing, and letting your faith move you to peace, purpose, and hope. Shalom is loving others, serving them, maintaining relationships with them, and being propelled into action and held to the highest possible standard of goodness.

It's fair to say that many of us need to change if we are to find shalom. We need to liberate ourselves from old values and perspectives, transform our consciousness, and seek a new orientation for our lives. Shalom is active, engaged, confronts and resists bad behavior, and works for the betterment of those in need. When we can manage to change as needed and to live this way of shalom, even for a moment, we pull each other up toward something bigger, wider, more beautiful.

Our lives have developed and become what they are over time, and if they are lacking, they cannot be quickly changed to ones that are whole and complete. Finding shalom is a journey. The journey is typically not easy, straightforward, or without risk. You will need to start from where you are and be clear about where you want to be. Listen to God. Base your decisions and actions on the great moral codes of the Bible and your sense of right and wrong. Take advantage of the improbable, difficult to explain events in your life that are examples of synchronicity. Profit from the experiences and learnings of individuals featured in this book. Demonstrate the love that is shalom.

I hope you enjoyed meeting the people in this book and that their examples have inspired you to undertake actions such as theirs to help you find shalom in your life. If so, think about which of their lives and learnings is most helpful for you. What if any insights about your life did their experiences present? What if any actions did they inspire you to take in your own life to foster shalom? What if anything should you do to change your life?

Congratulations for taking your first step by reading this book. What will be next for you?

I hope, in words from an unidentified source, that your life will be "nothing missing, nothing lacking, nothing broken . . . destroying that which binds to chaos." Remember what Jesus said in John 14:27: "Peace I leave with you; my peace I give you. I do not give to you as the world gives. Do not let your hearts be troubled and do not be afraid."

SHALOM

Appendix:
Restoring Peace Summary

The Bridges To Life restorative justice prison ministry was founded in 1998 to help victims of crime with their healing and reduce recidivism among released inmates by using small group discussions among victims and offenders to bring peace to those who have hurt or been hurt by another. It adopted guideline topics for these discussions. These topics became the chapters for *Restoring Peace*, which has become the centerpiece of the Bridges To Life curriculum. The following is a brief summary of each of these chapters.

Chapter 1: Bridges To Life

Restoring Peace is based on experiences of individuals who participated in a Bridges To Life prison program in which victims of serious crime engage in a process of peace and reconciliation with prison inmates who perpetrated such crimes against others.

Chapter 2: Faith

Belief in God is critical to the Bridges To Life experience and to peace and reconciliation. The Bible presents a great moral code, a process for change, and a basis for hope, but these are hollow without love. Peace and reconciliation will not occur without love of one another and God.

CHAPTER 3: STORIES

The Bridges To Life experience requires inmates and victims to tell their stories within their small groups at some time during the process. Telling their stories helps them consider the themes of their lives and sort out who they are. It sets the stage for them to accept responsibility and be accountable for their lives, and is a way of confessing their wrongdoings. The stories typically reveal suffering as well as times of happiness and well-being. Having people listen to them without hating, judging, or condemning is an empowering experience for all.

CHAPTER 4: RESPONSIBILITY

If a person causes conflict, hurt or a problem, they are responsible for what they did and its effects. Many influences typically cause us to do what we do, our actions usually cause several consequences, and they often affect many people.

People often do not take responsibility for their behavior that led to conflict or a problem, and offenders in the Bridges To Life program often have been masters of mishandling responsibility. We need to acknowledge our own actions and the consequences that resulted. Discerning the facts and accepting responsibility helps us understand what we've done, define who we are, identify what we need to change, and overcome the influences that are holding us where we are. And perhaps most important, accepting responsibility should trigger actions on our part to address the consequences for which we are responsible.

CHAPTER 5: ACCOUNTABILITY

Accountability flows from responsibility. Accountability means being answerable and implies a legal moral or other obligation to someone. It may arise from a formal relationship, such as one's obligation under the law or by specific written contract, or informally based on relationships and unstated expectations of those one cares about or loves. You are accountable if you are fully or partially responsible for a conflict, problem, or crime; your actions were inappropriate; you had a choice in the matter; and you have a duty of answering to someone. To be accountable, people should avoid running away from their situation, either physically, mentally, or emotionally, and instead acknowledge that they owe others an answer and take whatever actions are appropriate to maintain and approve their relationship.

Chapter 6: Confession

Confession means admitting we have been wrong and acknowledging or disclosing our misdeeds, faults, or sins to ourselves, to God, and to others. Confessing to others may involve revealing something to someone that the person doesn't already know; or communicating that we are accepting responsibility and being accountable for actions the other person is already aware of. Confession can begin a cycle of improvement in a relationship when one person responds to another person's confession. Most conflicts or problems involve some responsibility or fault on both sides, and when one person confesses, a repeating cycle begins and the door is open to reconciliation and a better relationship.

Regardless of when or how the confessions occur, doing so with humility will confirm the honesty, morality, strength, and dignity of those doing the confessing; lead to some level of confidence in the person receiving the confession; and in many cases begin a cycle of improvement in the relationship between them.

Chapter 7: Repentance

Repentance is a process in which a person's fundamental character and being, not just their surface behavior, become permanently different. It is not a one-time event, but is an ongoing daily, hourly change of attitude and life. When a person repents, deep remorse leads to a firm resolve to do better in the future and to become a new person. A key aspect of repentance is transforming one's focus from self to others. This requires listening to God, self, and others; empathizing with others by acknowledging your differences; controlling your emotions; putting yourself in the other person's shoes; embracing your choices; seeking God's help; and reviewing repentance as a journey.

CHAPTER 8: FORGIVENESS

Forgiveness is granting free pardon or giving up resentment for a hurt or debt against you. It does not change the past or the bad things that have happened, but it does change the present and can change the future. God loves all of us and is willing to forgive those who seek his forgiveness, and you can accept God's grace and his forgiveness as a way of forgiving yourself. If we are truly remorseful, we all want to be forgiven for our offenses and for hurting others. Forgiveness is an internal decision of the heart that does not require the offender to even know about it. And forgiveness should be unconditional and not dependent on the offender's action. Being forgiven by another is an essential part of the healing process, as forgiving another who has hurt you will free you from being consumed by anger, minimize any tendency you may have for vengeance or vindictiveness, and set the stage for restoring a relationship.

CHAPTER 9: RECONCILIATION

We often think of reconciliation as the coming together of two parties, but it means more and can address differences between people, within yourself, and between you and God. Reconciling with yourself can mean being at peace with yourself by recognizing who you are, acknowledging the conflicts within your being, and taking responsibility for what you have done or failed to do. Reconciling with God means being "friends" with Him. Reconciling with others means resolving your differences and coming to terms with them in any of a number of ways, depending on who you are, where you have been, and where you need to be. We can't force another to reconcile, but we can foster an environment for reconciliation and take a number of actions that make it more likely to happen.

Chapter 10: Restitution

Restitution is what you do to make amends or indemnify someone for a harm you have done to them. To the extent possible you give back or make right for the hurt. From a victim's perspective, forgiveness is necessary if restitution is to foster healing, and the restitution should be accepted with no expectation and with love. Offenders can make restitution to themselves by doing things that foster their wholeness as a person. They can make restitution to God by demonstrating their care for the small people of the world. Steps of the Bridges To Life process, such as accepting responsibility, being accountable, confessing, repenting, and reconciling naturally lead to making restitution to others.

Chapter 11: The Journey

Restoring Peace has given readers a roadmap for a journey to bring peace into their lives, but what they do is their decision. The important thing is to take the journey. They will not be alone. God will give them hope and with his help they can attain a better future.

Acknowledgments

John Sage, founder and CEO of the Bridges To Life (BTL) prison ministry, suggested I write a book about some of the people who have turned their lives around as a result of participating in the program. When I agreed, I thought that writing it would be a simple matter of telling a few short success stories. How wrong I was! Describing changed lives is one thing; explaining what caused the change, how it occurred, and what is to be learned from the experience is quite another. I needed help.

After considerable thought, I concluded that the lives I would be writing about are best described by the term "shalom," a multifaceted concept that envisions peace but also includes, among other things, good relationships among individuals. A level of shalom in my life greatly helped me in writing about the topic, as a number of individuals with whom I have a relationship willingly contributed their time, knowledge, and expertise to the project—an element of shalom for which I am deeply grateful to each of them.

First and foremost, I would like to thank John Sage and Jim Buffington, BTL's Chief Operating Officer. Experiences and learnings of BTL participants recommended by John and Jim are the essence of the book, and both individuals read draft manuscripts and provided great feedback concerning both factual and editorial matters. Equally important were Msgr. Frank Rossi and Rick Weintraub, a Messianic Jew. Each read several versions of the manuscript and provided invaluable feedback from their religious perspectives. I made several important additions and changes based on their recommendations, and their acceptance gave me a feeling of comfort in writing about issues that are not my expertise. Gay and John Van Osdall, Betty Gibson, George Dehan, and the staff of Mayfly Book

Design, especially Sean Strain, Julie Scheife and Jess LaGreca, provided much appreciated editorial and publishing assistance.

And always, many thanks to family and friends who continually encourage and support me in all my endeavors.

About the Author

Kirk Blackard holds a Bachelor of Arts degree in economics from Texas A&M University and a Doctor of Jurisprudence degree from the University of Texas School of Law. He is retired from a career with Shell Oil Company, where he held several senior executive positions in Houston and London. He has extensive conflict management and negotiation experience, has worked as a mediator and arbitrator, and served as chairman of the Board of the Bridges To Life restorative justice ministry that works in prisons to help victims heal their wounds and inmates change their lives. He is the author of *Restoring Peace*, the centerpiece of the BTL curriculum, and eleven other books. Kirk and Marcia, his wife of fifty-three years, live in Houston. They have two sons, two daughters-in-law and five grandchildren.

Bibliography

Introduction

Blackard, K. (2007). *Restoring Peace: Using Lessons from Prison to Mend Broken Relationships*. Trafford Publishing.

Ferguson, M. (1980). *The Aquarian Conspiracy: Personal and Social Transformation in the 1980s*. J. P. Tarcher, Inc.

Yoder, P. (2017). *Shalom: The Bible's Word for Salvation, Justice, and Peace*. Wipf and Stock Publishers.

Chapter 1: Listening to God

Beller, K and Chase (2008). *Great Peacemakers: True Stories from Around the World*. LTS Press.

Jaworski, J. (2011). *Synchronicity: The Inner Path of Leadership*. Berrett-Koehler Publishers.

Rushnell, Squire (2001). *When God Winks: How the Power of Coincidence Guides Your Life*. Howard Books.

Chapter 2: Discerning God's Will

Loyola, S. I. O. (1999). *The Spiritual Exercises of St. Ignatius: or Manresa*. Tan Classics.

Nouwen, H. J. M. (2015). *Discernment: Reading the Signs of Daily Life.* HarperOne.

CHAPTER 3: LOVING OTHERS

Lewis, C. S., (1960). *The Four Loves* Harcourt, Brace & Company.

CHAPTER 4: LIVING YOUR FAITH

Bass, D. C. (2009). *Practicing our Faith: A Way of Life for a Searching People.* John Wiley & Sons.

Levenson, R. J. (2020). *A Path to Wholeness: A Lenten Companion.* Church Publishing, Inc.

CHAPTER 5: CULTIVATING HOPE

Goodall, J., & Abrams, D. (2021). *The Book of Hope: A Survival Guide for an Endangered Planet.* Penguin UK.

Haring, Bernard (1972). *Hope is the Remedy.* Doubleday & Company, Inc.

Keller, T. (2021). *Hope in Times of Fear: The Resurrection and the Meaning of Easter.* Penguin.

Sampson, T. (2016). *A Message about Hope.* Lulu.com.

CHAPTER 6: LIVING FOR A PURPOSE

Frankl, V. E. (1985). *Man's Search for Meaning.* Simon and Schuster.

Strecher, V. J. (2016). *Life on Purpose: How Living for What Matters Most Changes Everything.* HarperCollins.

Warren, R. (2012). *The Purpose Driven Life: What on Earth Am I Here For?* Zondervan.

Chapter 7: Living by Moral Codes

Westley, D. (1984). *Morality and Its Beyond*. Twenty-Third Publications.

Chapter 8: Forgiving and Reconciling

Jones, L. G. (1995). *Embodying Forgiveness: A Theological Analysis*. Wm. B. Eerdmans Publishing.

Chapter 9: Serving Others

Lewis, C. S. (1952). *Mere Christianity*. HarperOne.

Mahaney, C. (2008). *Humility: True Greatness*. Multnomah.

Wiersbe, W. W., & Wiersbe, D. W. (2010). *10 Power Principles for Christian Service*. Baker Books.

Chapter 10: Maintaining Good Relationships

The Anatomy of Peace: Resolving the Heart of Conflict (2006). The Arbinger Institute (J. Ferrell, D. Boyce, et al.), San Francisco: Berrett-Koehler.

McLaren, K. (2013). *The Art of Empathy: A Complete Guide to Life's Most Essential Skill*. Sounds True.

Chapter 11: Changing Your Life

Conner, D. (1992). *Managing at the Speed of Change: How Resilient Managers Succeed and Prosper where Others Fail*. Villard Books.

Milkman, K. (2021). *How to Change: The Science of Getting from Where You Are to Where You Want to Be*. Random House.

Notes

1. Jaworski, J. (2011). Synchronicity: The Inner Path of Leadership. Berrett-Koehler Publishers, 190.

2. (www.brainyquote.com/ quotes/albert_einstein_574924)

3. www.britannica.com/biography/William-Temple

4. Nouwen, H. J. M. (2015). Discernment: Reading the Signs of Daily Life. HarperOne. 4

5. Nouwen, H. J. M. (2015). Discernment: Reading the Signs of Daily Life. 5

6. Nouwen, Discernment: Reading the Signs of Daily Life, 53.

7. Nouwen, Discernment: Reading the Signs of Daily Life, 83.

8. www.daisakuikeda.org

9. Frankl, V. E. (1985). Man's Search for Meaning. Simon and Schuster 9

10. Frankl, Man's Search for Meaning. 12

11. Frankl, Man's Search for Meaning. 15

12. Frankl, Man's Search for Meaning. 84

13. www.azquotes.com/author/8805-C_S_Lewis/tag/humility

14. The Anatomy of Peace: Resolving the Heart of Conflict (2006). The Arbinger Institute (J. Ferrell, D. Boyce, et al.), San Francisco: Berrett-Koehler. 253

15. Lewis, C. S. (1952). Mere Christianity. HarperOne. 56

www.ingramcontent.com/pod-product-compliance
Lightning Source LLC
Chambersburg PA
CBHW021641120626
46545CB00002B/646